MONEY
MAVEN

MANUAL

Helping you make
confident financial decisions

NICOLE BURDICK

ISBN: 979-8-9922675-1-8 (paperback)

ISBN: 979-8-9922675-2-5 (hardcover)

Book Cover by Amanda Peterson, AP Creative Co

Book Cover Photography by Emily Anne Merrill Photography

Book graphics by Kerstin Deneui, Kreative Heart Media

Illustrations by Nicole Burdick

Interior formatting by Jen Henderson, Wild Words Formatting

"We should appreciate the women on whose shoulders we stand— women who said what we say now, but at a time when society wasn't ready to listen."

—*Justice Ruth Bader Ginsburg*

———————— ✦ ————————

This book is dedicated to the women who paved the way for the rights we as women now hold: the ability to own our own property, to access credit without a male co-signer, the legal entitlement to equal pay regardless of our gender.

In particular, I want to honor the late Justice Ruth Bader Ginsburg. Ruth, you most certainly left tracks, and the world is far better for your having lived—for both men and women. Your voice is missed, but your words will never be forgotten.

ACKNOWLEDGEMENTS

This book would not exist without the love, support, and encouragement of so many people who believed in me and this work. On the days I wanted to quit, when I questioned whether I had anything to say that hadn't already been said, and wondered why I ever decided to take on this project—you carried me through!

To my husband, Josh, who has supported me in all my crazy commitments and helped carve out time in our already busy schedule so I could work on this book—I'm lucky to call you mine, and so grateful that you chose me and continue to choose us.

To my daughter, Abby, who is never afraid to ask, "Mom, are you doing what you're supposed to be doing?"—keeping me on track when my ADHD kicks in. Your goofiness and quick wit make me smile on days when I want to cry.

To my son, Andy, thank you for all your snuggles and kisses and kind words when I was stressed about writing, even if (as you reminded me) "Well, Mom, it was your choice to do it."

To my friends who encouraged me when I wanted to quit (especially Meg!) and my beta readers—thank you for your feedback and support.

To my incredible writing coach, Jocelyn, who guided me from start to finish and talked me out of quitting more than once. Your patience and expertise were invaluable, and I don't know how I'd be crossing the finish line without your guidance.

And finally, to every single person who asked, "How's your book coming along?"—thank you for holding me accountable, even when my motivation fizzled. You made it impossible to quit, and for that I am thankful.

This book is as much yours as it is mine. Thank you for being part of this journey.

TABLE OF CONTENTS

FOREWORD

I have been in the finance field for more than three decades, and for the first time I see someone blending money matters with life matters so seamlessly and so caringly.

In *The Money Maven Manual*, Nicole Burdick does something extraordinary—she brings together the technical side of money and the human side of life. She understands that financial success is not just about spreadsheets and statements, but about values, mindset, and the stories we carry from childhood into adulthood.

This book is both practical and personal. It will help you uncover your money mindset, rewrite unhelpful beliefs, and build new habits that align with the life you truly want. Nicole guides you with clarity and compassion, offering tools that empower rather than overwhelm.

What sets this book apart is Nicole herself. She writes not only as a seasoned financial advisor, but as a woman who has walked alongside countless others on their journeys toward peace and confidence with money. Her approach is honest, empathetic, and deeply empowering.

By the time you finish, you won't just understand your finances better—you'll understand yourself better. And that is the true gift of this book:

freedom, clarity, and the confidence to design a financial life in alignment with your values.

As you turn the page, be ready for more than information—be ready for transformation. May this book be a turning point in your journey, and may it bless every decision you make from this day forward.

Dr. Betty® Uribe
Former Managing Director, JPMorgan Chase
United Nations Ambassador for Peace and Human Rights
Author *#Values: The Secret to Top-Level Performance in Business & Life*

INTRODUCTION

Welcome, friend. I'm so glad you're here. Whether you picked up this book because you're curious, motivated, or maybe even a little overwhelmed by your financial life, you're in the right place.

Before we dive in, let me introduce myself. I'm Nicole Burdick, a financial advisor since 2014 and the author of this book. For over a decade, I have helped women take control of their money and make choices that align with their values.

I wrote *The Money Maven Manual* because financial advice should feel personal, practical, and empowering—not overwhelming, condescending, or one-size-fits-all. This isn't just another money book. It's a guide to help you understand yourself better so you can make financial decisions with clarity and confidence.

Let me tell you a little secret: managing your money isn't just about dollars and cents—it's about knowing yourself. It's about understanding your habits, your values, and the stories you tell yourself about money. And, most importantly, it's about giving yourself the tools and confidence to design a financial life you love.

The clients I work with typically want help, not because they don't understand money, but because they feel disconnected from it. They say things like, "I'm just not good with numbers," "My partner always handles the finances," or "I feel guilty about spending on myself." These aren't just passing thoughts; they're deeply held beliefs shaped by experiences, culture, and sometimes fear.

One of the most important lessons from this last decade is this: personal finance isn't just personal—it's emotional. And while there's no shortage of advice about saving, budgeting, and investing, there's a gap when it comes to connecting the practical with the personal. That's what this book is here to do.

Think of this book like a map. We'll start by pinpointing your "You Are Here" spot—an honest look at where you're starting, with no shame or judgment. Throughout the book, we'll take one step at a time, each time doing "the next right thing." The path is yours, but I'll walk it with you.

YOUR ROAD MAP

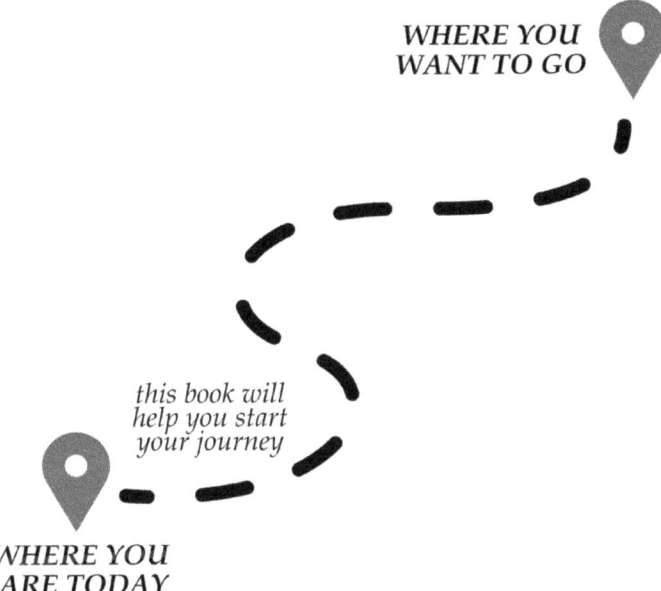

WHERE YOU WANT TO GO

this book will help you start your journey

WHERE YOU ARE TODAY

You'll find exercises throughout this book designed to help you reflect, plan, and take action. Think of it as a conversation—one where you get to dream big, set goals, and build a plan that fits who you are and what matters most. My hope is that you'll come away not just with practical tools, but with a sense of clarity and confidence that carries over into every corner of your life.

I know that finances can feel overwhelming, but you're not alone. You have what it takes to thrive, and you're about to prove it to yourself. Let's get started—your future is waiting.

"Money is only a tool.
It will take you wherever
you wish, but it will not
replace you as the driver."

—Ayn Rand

Chapter 1

MASTERING YOUR MONEY MINDSET

Money Values

I'm a big fan of learning about money from people who are older than me, who can share from the experience that they've accumulated over the years. I love hearing their stories of how they got to where they are and how they overcame challenging circumstances. I've been able to apply much of their wisdom and experience to my own life.

I've also realized that while there's a lot to learn about how others have achieved *their* financial goals, no one else can chart the path for *me* to accomplish *mine*. I can't stitch their stories together to chart a perfect path. I can learn a lot from them, but, at some point, I have to make my own way.

As a perfectionist, the idea of forging my own financial journey without a clear set of instructions is intimidating—but less so when I realize that I can let my values be my guide.

Your values are the driving force behind everything you do: the goals you set, how you use your time, how you spend your money, who you cultivate relationships with, and how you approach your work life—every single decision you make.

At least, they are in an ideal world.

But too often we allow other people's voices to be louder than our own, drowning out what we intuitively know. These voices could be those of family members, teachers, friends, coworkers, or random people we follow on the internet. Whether intentionally or unintentionally, solicited or unsolicited, they are projecting their values onto us—and we may not even realize it.

Consider the following well-intentioned advice you may have heard:

"Get in on real estate now. Renting is a waste of money."

"Wait to buy a house until you have 20% saved."

"Don't make extra payments on low-interest debt."

"Dedicate every dollar you have to becoming debt-free."

Chances are, you've heard variations of the above or have other examples of conflicting advice from people in your life. It's all too easy to internalize these messages.

The problem isn't that these pieces of advice are entirely wrong. In fact, they can be correct for the right person, in the right situation, at the right time. But how do you know what advice to follow or what financial path is right for you?

The key is to filter every financial decision through your own clearly defined personal values—we'll define these in just a bit.

Keep in mind that values are different from goals. You won't find "pay off my credit card debt" on a list of values.

Paying off your credit cards is not a value in itself; it's a reflection of a deeper value. That value may be simplicity, where you prefer not to juggle multiple credit cards with varying interest rates and payment schedules. It could be freedom, defined by your desire to avoid the feeling of owing anything to anyone. Or perhaps it's optimization, as you aim to save money by securing better interest rates through maintaining a high credit score and low debt levels. In other words, paying off your credit cards is the "what," while your values are the "why."

When you root your goals in your values, they gain power. It's so much more powerful to say, "Paying this debt off is important to me because I want more freedom and simplicity in my life," versus "I should pay off my credit cards because that's the responsible thing to do." It's important to note that the word "should" can be a signal that you are experiencing a conflict between what someone else has told you and what you actually believe and value.

> **When you root your goals in your values, they gain power.**

When it comes to making financial decisions, there is no universal "right" or "wrong." What's right for someone else might not be right for you. Don't let anyone "should" all over you. We all hold different personal values, and you won't be living in alignment with your values if you try to copy what someone else is doing.

Defining Your Core Values

Taking the time to thoughtfully define your core values is a powerful step toward financial empowerment. It helps make sure your money choices reflect what truly matters to you—not societal pressures or others' expectations. When your financial life aligns with your values, you gain clarity, confidence, and control, creating a foundation for decisions that support both your goals and your well-being.

I invite you to take the time to read through the following list of values and circle the ones that best resonate with you.

CORE VALUES

Adventure	Equality	Loyalty
Autonomy	Experience	Minimalism
Balance	Faith	Nature
Collaboration	Family	Options
Comfort	Fitness	Originality
Community	Flexibility	Preparedness
Consistency	Freedom	Privacy
Contributing	Friends	Responsibility
Control	Fun	Safety
Convenience	Generosity	Service
Creativity	Grace	Simplicity
Culture	Health	Spontaneity
Dependability	Hospitality	Stability
Diversity	Inclusivity	Stewardship
Education	Independence	Sustainability
Empowerment	Justice	Travel
Entertainment	Literacy	Variety

Now that you have a sense of which values you identify with, go back over the list and put a star next to the five values that matter most to you.

These are your core values—the framework for making choices about how you spend your time, money, and energy. Let's dive deeper into what those values mean to you and why they're important.

Exercise: My Core Values

Core Value #1:

What this word means to me:

Why this is important:

Core Value #2:

What this word means to me:

Why this is important:

Core Value #3:

What this word means to me:

Why this is important:

Core Value #4:

What this word means to me:

Why this is important:

Core Value #5:

What this word means to me:

Why this is important:

Core Values Examples

In case you feel a little stuck or just need some inspiration, here are a few examples of core values.

Core Value #1: Independence

What this means to me: Using my time, money, and energy how I want to.

Why this is important: Having independence allows me to have an idea and act on it without asking anyone's permission. It makes it easier for me to take care of myself and allows me to help others spontaneously.

Core Value #2: Contributing

What this means to me: Using my resources (time, money, skills, and personal connections) to help others.

Why this is important: I've received help many times throughout my life, and it's important to me to pay it forward to others. I also feel called to love and serve the people God has placed in my life.

Money Mindset

Over the years, I've learned a lot about money and how it works. I've read countless personal finance books, listened to hours of podcasts about money management, and attended quite a few financial conferences.

But my pursuit of financial knowledge was never about gaining more information. The truth is, my efforts have all been in the pursuit of financial peace.

Financial anxiety has been a constant thread in my life, woven through childhood and into early adulthood. It showed up in hand-me-downs and clearance-rack clothes that never quite fit. It was there when I battled severe acne but couldn't afford a dermatologist, let alone the products they might recommend. And it surfaced again when friends invited me to summer camp, and I didn't know if I could go because my parents couldn't cover the cost the way theirs could.

I wasn't learning about money to become rich—I just wanted to live a normal life without thinking about money all the time. I wanted to be able to buy clothes that fit, see a doctor if I needed to, and spend time with friends.

Along my financial learning journey, I stumbled across something called "money mindset." Learning "how to think" didn't feel as productive as learning "how to do," so I got straight to the "real" work of making and managing money.

I set financial goals and worked towards them. I graduated college, bought a home with my husband, and we worked our tails off to pay off our student loans.

I was checking all the boxes, eager to finally reach the financial peace I thought awaited me. But every time I reached what should have felt like the finish line—the pot of gold at the end of the rainbow—the peace never came. I kept wondering what I was missing.

That's when I returned to the topic of money mindset. I realized I should have started my financial journey here! My money mindset was holding me back financially and also keeping me from enjoying the money I already had. I wanted peace, not just progress. To find it, I had to examine the beliefs underneath my habits. That is where money mindset begins.

Your money mindset is shaped by how you were raised, your lived experiences, and cultural influences. It is the source of the beliefs, attitudes, and emotions that shape your relationship with money and plays a significant role in determining your financial success.

In its most simple form, your money mindset tells you what you can and cannot accomplish financially and how you should feel about money.

Let's explore some common money mindsets and how they impact your relationship with money.

Scarcity

A scarcity mindset is very common. It is characterized by the belief that money is limited and by a fear of not having enough for tomorrow, even if you have enough for today. This is the money mindset I lived with most of my life.

My lack of peace around money wasn't based on how much debt I carried or how much I was earning. It was my scarcity mindset that kept me stuck.

It led me to save more and spend less, fueled by the fear that there might not be enough. But I was chasing a feeling, not a number, and no amount of spending cuts or money in the bank account would grant me that elusive peace of mind.

Here are some ways that scarcity mindset shows up:

- **Earning potential:** A person with a scarcity mindset may believe that money is hard to come by and may miss opportunities to increase their earning potential. A scarcity mindset can cause someone to focus so much on preserving what they have that they overlook or avoid taking risks that could lead to greater income or growth.

- **Spending habits:** A person with a scarcity mindset is more likely to hoard money and be overly cautious with spending. The spending they do engage in may be infused with anxiety, as they are worried that money they spend today may result in not having enough tomorrow.

- **Investing/Saving:** A person with a scarcity mindset may invest too conservatively out of fear. For long-term funds, such as retirement savings, investing too conservatively may result in not having enough income in retirement.

Overcoming a scarcity mindset starts by tracking what you *do* have—your income, resources, and support systems—rather than focusing only on what's missing. Build confidence by setting aside small, consistent amounts in savings, even if it's just $25 a month to start. Practice generosity in low-cost ways, like sharing time or encouragement, to remind yourself there *is* enough. Balance means planning for the future while also allowing yourself to enjoy life now without guilt.

YOLO

YOLO, or "You Only Live Once," is a mindset that prioritizes experiences and immediate gratification over long-term planning. Rather than delaying gratification and preparing for setbacks (like someone with a scarcity mindset), a person with a YOLO mindset avoids it altogether, believing it could all disappear at any moment. There are many reasons people develop a YOLO approach to money. For many, social media plays a large role. We see influencers promoting luxury vacations, concerts, high-end brands, and expensive health products in the name of "living my best life."

Sometimes traumatic events can also trigger this mindset. The sudden death of a loved one or a scary medical diagnosis can make someone question why they should save for a future they might never see.

Economic uncertainty or distrust in financial institutions can further reinforce a YOLO mindset. Saving for the future seems futile if the value of money feels uncertain or if those savings could be lost due to economic downturns.

While the YOLO mindset can inspire a sense of freedom and adventure, it has significant implications for how individuals approach earning, spending, and saving.

- **Earning Potential:** A YOLO mindset can boost earning potential by encouraging risk-taking and passion-driven career moves. However, it can also lead to impulsive decisions and instability.

- **Spending:** The idea that life is short and should be lived to the fullest can lead to impulsive spending habits, as individuals may be more inclined to splurge on extravagant purchases or indulge in expensive activities without considering the consequences. Someone with a YOLO mindset is more likely to find themselves in debt, as they prioritize immediate enjoyment at the expense of their future financial stability.

- **Saving/Investing:** The idea of saving or investing for the future is pretty low on the priority list for someone with a YOLO mindset. The focus is on making the most of today, as tomorrow might never come.

Overcoming a YOLO money mindset begins with recognizing that while it's important to be present in the moment, your future self deserves consideration too. Balance is the key to ensuring that how you live your life now doesn't compromise your ability to enjoy life in the future.

Avoidance

Avoidance is a mindset where you struggle to engage with your money. You may be aware of the reason you're avoiding it, or it may be a subconscious block that you constantly come up against.

You might find yourself stuck in a cycle that looks something like this:

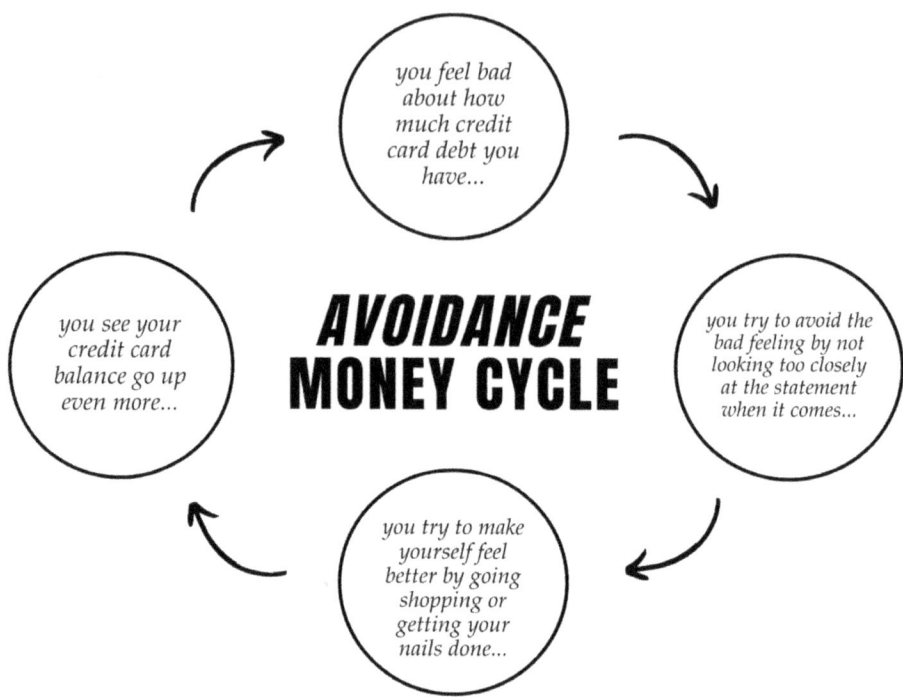

Everyone's avoidance cycle is different—perhaps you've put off logging into your investment account, signing up for your 401(k) at work, or getting life insurance. Maybe it's your salary—you know you've been earning less than you should be, and you know you need to negotiate a raise. You feel embarrassed that you haven't done it already, yet continue avoiding the task.

Whatever the thing is that you're avoiding, the longer you put it off, the greater the resistance—keeping you stuck until you work through the emotions underneath. You may need support from a coach or a therapist—don't be afraid to ask for help! If it's any consolation, it is *extremely* common for high-achieving women to find themselves in this situation. You are not alone!

Let's take a look at how money avoidance can manifest in different areas of personal finance.

- **Earning Potential:** A money avoidance mindset can hold back your earning potential by keeping you in the dark. When you avoid looking at your finances—like your income, expenses, or pricing—you miss key opportunities to adjust, grow, or ask for more. Without clarity, it's easy to undercharge, stay underpaid, or overlook ways to increase your income.

- **Spending:** Money avoidance often manifests as overspending. Someone struggling with money avoidance may resist using a budgeting app or tracking their spending. While the ambiguity causes anxiety, it feels less scary than facing their finances directly.

- **Debt:** Avoidance often leads to piling up debt or struggling to pay it down, since creating a payoff plan requires facing the numbers directly.

- **Investing/Saving:** Fear of making the wrong investment decision can cause procrastination, resulting in missed opportunities such as company 401(k) matches. Avoidance may also leave funds uninvested or in poorly performing investments due to lack of monitoring.

The key to overcoming money avoidance is to understand what you are *really* avoiding and to practice self-compassion along the way. Most money avoidance has fear or shame at its root, so facing your fears and giving yourself grace is essential.

Abundance

An abundance mindset is the opposite of a scarcity mindset. It's the belief that there is enough and that resources are plentiful. People with this mindset focus on possibilities and potential for growth instead of limitations and constraints.

They tend to be optimistic and confident in their ability to create wealth and financial success. They are more likely to take calculated risks and pursue new opportunities for earning more money. They also tend to be more generous and open to giving.

Here's what living with an abundance mindset can look like:

- **Earning Potential:** Because they believe there will always be enough money and that financial opportunities will come their way, they are more open to recognizing and pursuing these opportunities.

- **Spending:** They are comfortable spending their money, trusting that more will come and that it isn't a limited resource. They aren't necessarily excessive spenders, but the spending they do engage in does not cause them anxiety.

- **Investing/Saving:** Rather than focusing on potential losses, they see opportunities for growth. They're more likely to set long-term goals, contribute consistently, and make financial decisions based on possibility rather than fear—leading to a more strategic and optimistic approach to building wealth.

Having an abundance mindset is a great thing—it helps you stay focused on growth and possibility. But if you only look at the upside, you might miss some real risks, like job loss, health issues, or an unexpected dip in your business.

That's why it's important to have some safety nets in place, like emergency savings and the right insurance. It's not about being fearful—it's about being wise.

An abundance mindset is the healthiest of the four because it frees you from fear and limitation. When it's paired with practical safety nets, it becomes the foundation for both financial peace and long-term growth.

Changing Your Mindset

Developing an abundance mindset takes time and effort, as you rewrite a story that you've spent your whole life living.

Here are a few strategies that can help:

1. **Change Your Language:** Pay attention to how you talk about money. Phrases like "I can't afford it" or "I don't have enough" reinforce a scarcity mindset. Instead, try saying, "I choose to spend my money in ways that support the life I want to live."

2. **Define "Enough"**: Clarify what "enough" looks like for you—not as an unattainable feeling, but as a tangible goal. Having a clear definition reduces the endless pursuit of "more" and brings focus to what truly matters.

3. **Embrace Uncertainty**: Accept that certainty is unattainable. Instead of fearing the unknown, see it as a space for growth and possibility, empowering you to make confident decisions.

4. **Practice Gratitude:** Cultivate an attitude of gratitude for the money and resources you already have. Gratitude rewires your brain to notice abundance and strengthens a deeper sense of security.

5. **Reframe Your Limiting Beliefs:** Challenge limiting beliefs about money. For example, instead of thinking, "I will never be able to afford that," shift to "What steps can I take to afford that in the future?"

6. **Be Open to Opportunities:** When you believe that there are financial opportunities out there, you're more likely to see and act on them.

7. **Practice Generosity:** Sharing your resources, even in small ways, helps foster a sense of abundance and generosity.

8. **Learn about Money:** Educate yourself on money management, budgeting, and investing. Viewing money as a tool rather than a source of fear empowers you to make informed decisions.

9. **Surround Yourself with Positive Influences:** Spend time with people who have a healthy money mindset and who can support you on your journey.

CHAPTER WRAP-UP

Key Takeaways

- If we don't define our own money values, we end up living by someone else's.

- Our money mindset is not fixed—we have the power to change it.

- An abundance mindset is the healthiest to operate from, but it works best when paired with practical safeguards like savings and insurance.

Key Action

- Define your core values.

- **Track where your money goes for one month** and notice whether your spending reflects your stated values.

- **Start a gratitude list focused on money and resources** (big or small) to train your brain to see abundance.

Journal Prompt

- Have you ever followed someone else's financial advice that didn't feel quite right for you? What happened?

- Which mindset do you most relate to right now—Scarcity, YOLO, Avoidance, or Abundance? Why?

- What's something you've been avoiding financially? What emotions come up when you think about tackling it?

- Describe a time you made a money decision that truly aligned with your values. What made it feel right?

- Imagine your future self five years from now—calm, confident, and living in alignment with your values. What does she want you to start doing today?

Chapter 2

MONEY STORY

One of the foundational building blocks of your money mindset is your money story. Your money story is formed in childhood, beginning as young as the age of 3 or 4, and continues to develop and evolve as you grow up.

Your money story was shaped by watching your parents talk (or not talk) about money and seeing how they made financial decisions. As a child, you sought to make meaning of the world, to understand why things happened. You were like a little scientist, forming your own "if…then" experiments to anticipate outcomes and be prepared.

Perhaps you learned "If Mom spends money on herself, then Dad gets mad," which led you to hide your spending to avoid conflict with your partner. Perhaps you grew up in a family that didn't set financial boundaries and internalized the belief, "If I don't give family money when they ask, that means I'm selfish."

This story unfolds in the day-to-day, but it can also be shaped by jarring events such as a parent's job loss, a death, or a divorce. Your extended family, religious community, culture, gender, social class—every aspect of what formed you—contributes to your money story, whether you're aware of it or not. It influences your money decisions more than financial literacy.

Here's the thing about money stories: they're not inherently good or bad. They're usually a mix of helpful and harmful beliefs. Often, the money story you internalized as a child was necessary for survival. Taking the time to understand your money story as an adult allows you to consciously rewrite the parts that no longer serve you.

Real Stories, Real Impact

To give you an idea of how money stories are created—and how they can shape our financial decisions later in life—here are three people's stories, including one of my own.

The Giving Jar

When I was little, my crafty mom had my younger brother and me make money jars to visually show how we could separate money for spending, saving, and giving. We made the jars by using old tin cans and decorating them with leftover fabric. I chose a fabric that was bright red and used glittery gold puffy paint to make the can look like a crown with jewels. My giving jar was a bedazzled work of art.

One Sunday morning, we brought the money in our giving jars to church to place in the offering plate. I brought what I thought was the "right" amount—10% of my allowance. I was excited to do a good thing by giving money to my church and eagerly poured the contents of my beautiful can into the offering plate. I remember feeling proud.

Then it was my brother's turn. He didn't follow the 10% rule. He joyfully put all of his money into the plate, not just a portion. My immediate thought was, "Why wasn't I generous enough to give all of my money? Why am I so selfish?" The joy faded and was replaced by shame. I told myself I must be greedy for keeping any money for myself.

At that moment, part of my money story was written: "Real generosity means giving everything you can and not keeping any for yourself." This story has played out throughout my life whenever I see a need I could meet—sometimes with financial means, sometimes with my time or energy. It has often led me to either overcommit or feel guilty when I set a boundary.

The Missionary's Daughter

Sarah grew up in a missionary family that didn't talk much about money at home. When money was tight, they would pray and ask God to provide. They knew they had been called to missionary life and never considered changing careers for a more financially comfortable lifestyle.

Her parents' choices were deeply rooted in their values and convictions and may have been right for them. But for Sarah, the money story she internalized was: "If you want to live out your faith, you shouldn't think about money when choosing a vocation." She came to believe that if she did care about money or evaluated careers based on income potential, she must care more about money than her faith. She didn't believe she could be a good Christian and earn good money. That belief kept her from pursuing jobs with real earning potential.

The Cynical Saver

Jennifer was a natural saver from a young age, skipping candy, nail polish, and makeup to save up for bigger purchases. At thirteen, she set a goal of saving $300 for an iPod. For months, she gave every dollar she received to her mom to deposit in her savings account, including her allowance and birthday money. The allure of having "1,000 songs in her pocket" kept her motivated.

When the day came to head to the store to cash in on all her hard work, Jennifer made a devastating discovery: her mom hadn't deposited the money—she had spent it all. Every single penny. Her mom promised to pay it back but was never able to. Jennifer was heartbroken.

As an adult, Jennifer was unable to save, leaving her anxious and embarrassed. But her inability to save wasn't due to a lack of desire. The iPod incident had taught her: "Money saved is not safe. If I want to be in control of my money, I should spend it." This is a common response for people who have had money stolen from them or borrowed and not repaid.

Money stories can't be fixed with financial literacy; they can only be changed through personal awareness. Untangling the money stories we've internalized can be a complicated process. It would be easier if these stories were fully false and could simply be tossed out. However, our money stories often contain nuggets of truth that reflect core beliefs we still hold.

To move forward, we need to break down these stories. Keep what serves us and let go of what doesn't. A great tool to help rewrite our stories is by practicing positive money affirmations, which we'll explore next.

Money Affirmations

What's one thing Oprah, Lady Gaga, and Selena Gomez all have in common?

They're all extremely talented and wealthy, but they also all believe in the power of positive affirmations—a practice that helped them achieve their remarkable levels of success.

Affirmations are short, powerful statements that help you consciously take control of and shape your thoughts. Our minds aren't designed to be empty. We can't simply eliminate negative money beliefs and move on. We need to create new mental pathways.

Imagine an old dirt road that's been driven for years, leaving deep ruts where the tires have repeatedly traveled. To escape those ruts, new tracks must be formed, or a vehicle will get yanked right back into the old tracks. When it comes to rewriting your money story, we form new tracks by using money affirmations.

Take some time to reflect on the mindset you want to adopt around money, then write out your own money affirmations. These statements may be aspirational, but they should also feel realistic. To be truly effective, they need to be short, meaningful, and written in the present tense.

Here are some examples to get you started, and there's space at the end of the chapter for writing your own.

Example Money Affirmations

- I am a money maven.
- I am growing my financial confidence.
- I have the power to change my financial position.
- I am a steward of the blessings I receive.
- I am capable of making wise financial decisions.
- Money is a tool I use to live out my values.
- Money gives me options.
- Investing in myself allows me to invest in others.
- I am growing my income so I can grow my impact.
- I deserve financial peace.
- I boldly pursue my money goals.
- Understanding my money empowers my financial independence.
- My core values drive my financial decisions.
- I have all I need to work toward my money goals.
- I use the money I receive to make the world a better place.
- I am improving my relationship with money.
- Now is the time to commit to my goals.
- I am organized and responsible with my money.
- I am moving in the right direction with my money.

Write your affirmations down and place them somewhere you'll see them. Read them out loud every day. Yes, it might feel silly. Do it anyway!

These affirmations will help you override the negative self-talk in your head.

CHAPTER WRAP-UP

Key Takeaways

- We all have money stories that shape our money behaviors.

- **Your money story isn't fixed—you have the power to rewrite it.** Awareness of the beliefs you inherited allows you to keep what serves you and release what doesn't.

- **Financial literacy alone can't change your money story.** Real transformation comes from personal reflection, affirmations, and intentional mindset shifts.

Key Action

- Write down the money messages you absorbed growing up and reflect on how they show up in your life today.

- Talk through your discoveries with a coach, therapist, or accountability partner for added clarity and encouragement.

- Write and regularly practice money affirmations that align with your new mindset.

Journal Prompt

- What is your earliest memory related to money?

- What messages did you hear about money growing up? How did your family manage money?

- What money story did you internalize as a result of these messages?

- What parts of this story have served you well, either in your past or now?

- What parts of your money story no longer serve you?

Chapter 3

WHERE'S MY MONEY?

It's Common to Feel Scattered

When I talk with women about what stresses them out about money, they rarely mention asset allocation, risk tolerance, or investment objectives. They don't say they wish they had a formal comprehensive financial plan. Nope.

Want to know what the common stressors are?
- Not knowing how much they have saved for retirement
- Not knowing where their accounts are
- Not understanding their investment options, or which ones to choose
- Feeling scattered or unsure of where to start

I can't tell you how many incredibly competent women say things like:
- "I feel like I should know this by now."
- "I'd be so embarrassed if anyone found out I still haven't [fill in the blank] at my age."
- "You'd think that since I work in [insert professional industry], I'd understand this stuff."

Let me start this chapter by saying: If you identify with any of these feelings, *you are not alone.*

We all went through school and were launched into the workforce without ever getting an "Adulting 101" class. It's not your fault you don't know what you were never taught.

It's normal to feel overwhelmed—or even paralyzed—by the idea of doing something you've never done before. In this chapter, I'll teach you how to track down where all of your money is and create a system that lets you easily monitor it at any time in the future with minimal effort on your part!

Tracking down your money and organizing it isn't rocket science, but seeing the numbers (your debt, your bank accounts, your investment accounts) for the first time can trigger a range of emotions, like stepping on a scale and seeing your weight. As these feelings arise, whatever they are, take a moment to sit with them and write them out. Glossing over your feelings will keep the work in your head, limiting its impact. Sitting with your feelings and working through them engages your heart, helping you actively connect with your money. Processing these emotions enables you to leave the past in the past and move forward.

Before diving into the logistics, it's important to pause and acknowledge where you are emotionally. Feeling scattered isn't just a logistics problem—it's often a sign that this area of life feels tangled, overwhelming, or even shameful. The goal isn't to master everything overnight; it's simply to begin with one small, steady step at a time.

Here are a few examples of how others have felt when they think about looking at their numbers:

"I'm scared to add up all my debts because I don't think I'll ever be able to pay them off. It feels easier to live with uncertainty than to face it. But I think that's why I'm still stuck."

"I'm proud of how hard I work and how much money I make, but when I look at my bank account and my 401(k), I feel like I have nothing to show for it."

Once you've had a moment to acknowledge those feelings, the next step is about taking action—gently, and at your own pace. This isn't about judgment; it's about getting the clarity you deserve.

Creating a Financial Snapshot

To gain clarity around where all your money is, we're going to create a financial snapshot by writing down on paper the balance of every single account. We do this manually for two reasons: First, the physical act of writing engages the brain in a way that typing does not. Second, by using a physical worksheet or notebook, you're less likely to open a text or end up on Instagram. (Hello, ADHD!)

This financial snapshot marks the starting point for the next stage of your financial journey. Like any journey, you can't get where you're going without knowing where you're starting. This is the "before" to your "after," the "You are here" pin at the trailhead.

This journey may feel daunting, but you can do it! One day you'll look back and feel so proud of yourself. Again, please don't skip over the feelings—take time to journal them so you can fully appreciate the progress you've made.

Go ahead and use the following worksheet and list every financial asset you have under the "What I Own" section. This may include checking and savings accounts, as well as CDs, retirement accounts, and cash-value life insurance if you have these. You can also include assets like your car, your laptop, and your house if you're a homeowner.

Next, list every debt you have, along with its interest rate, under the "What I Owe" section. Include credit card balances, student loans, car loans, mortgage, etc. You can usually find the interest rate by logging into your account online or checking your most recent statement. If you're unsure, call the lender directly and ask—they're required to tell you. Knowing the rate will help you understand what each loan is costing you.

FINANCIAL SNAPSHOT

ASSETS
(what I own)

LIABILITIES
(what I owe)

CASH
Checking: _____
Savings: _____
CD: _____
Money: _____
Market: _____
Other: _____

INVESTMENTS
401k: _____
IRA: _____
Roth IRA: _____
Brokerage: _____
Other: _____

PROPERTY:
House: _____
Car: _____
Other: _____
Other: _____

Mortgage: *Balance / Interest*
Car Loan(s): _____
Student Loan(s): _____
Student Loan(s): _____
Student Loan (s): _____
Credit Card(s): _____
Credit Card(s): _____
Other: _____

As you review these numbers, you may feel some resentment toward people who negatively contributed to your current financial situation—for example by giving you bad advice or taking advantage of you in some way. That's completely valid, but staying stuck in blame won't help you move forward. Even if others contributed to where you are now, *you* have the power to shape what comes next. It might take support from a therapist or coach to process those emotions, and that's okay. Do what you need to do to keep taking steps toward a better financial future.

If you're feeling great after completing this exercise, that's awesome—go you! If you're staring at a negative number or find yourself in the "I have so much debt I want to cry" camp, know that I'm sending you a big hug and reminding you: you're going to be okay. You've got this!

Reminder: your worth is not defined by measuring your assets against your liabilities. You have God-given value simply for being you and have so much to offer that can't be measured by dollar signs. Your life experiences, the skills you've developed, the education you've earned, and the inner work you've done—these things are just as valuable, if not more so, than your finances. This is why we use the term "Financial Snapshot" rather than "Net Worth Statement."

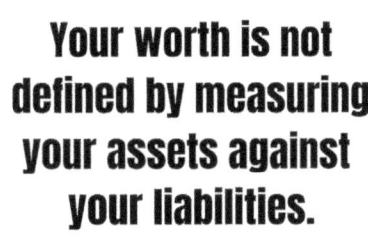

Your worth is not defined by measuring your assets against your liabilities.

Congratulations, my friend—by facing your numbers head-on, you've taken a HUGE step toward mastering your money. Be proud of yourself! Now, let's make it easier for you to maintain this mastery.

There's an App for That

Keeping track of your money is much easier if you use a budgeting tool that automatically connects all of your bank accounts, credit cards, and investments. These apps can both show all your balances in one place and help you monitor your transactions and spending patterns as well (which we'll cover in the next chapter).

Here are some key features to keep in mind when choosing an app:

- **Is it free?** If it's free, the app may be selling your data, withholding the best features for the paid version, or bombarding you with ads.

- **Does it load your transactions automatically?** Tools requiring manual uploads can be time-consuming and harder to maintain.

- **Can you customize budget categories?** This is especially helpful if you manage money differently than others or want to track specific spending areas in your life.

- **Is it mobile-friendly?** An app that's easy to use on the go will help you stay consistent.

- **Does it allow you to split transactions?** For example, if you buy groceries and clothes at the same store, you'll want to separate those purchases.

- As far as security considerations, make sure the app you choose uses **a two-factor password**. Access should be **read only**, meaning you don't have the option to move money between accounts.

I'm hesitant to share specific app suggestions, as they come and go all the time, but at the time of this publication I'm a big fan of Monarch Money and have heard good things about *You Need a Budget* (aka YNAB). Once you've chosen an app, connect all the accounts listed in your financial snapshot—checking, savings, retirement, credit cards, and other loans. For items that don't sync automatically, such as your car or laptop, you'll need to enter them manually.

Having everything in one place provides a clear visual of where your money is. Every time you review it, you're engaging with your finances. This makes it easier to track your progress and, hopefully, sleep better at night.

One last note I'll make is to keep in mind that there won't be a perfect app with zero frustrations—you'll need to reconnect links and deal with occasional tech hiccups. Know that the best app for you is one that you're able to commit to and use consistently.

CHAPTER WRAP-UP

Key Takeaways

- If you feel scattered, overwhelmed, or embarrassed, you're not alone!

- No matter how you got to where you are today, it's up to you to take the next step forward.

- Identifying where you're at by knowing your numbers will help you figure out your next steps.

Key Actions

- Complete your financial snapshot worksheet.

- Begin using a budgeting app to sync all your accounts in one place.

- Consolidate accounts (such as savings accounts at multiple banks or 401(k)s from past employers) when possible to simplify your financial management.

Journal Prompts

- How do you feel when looking at your financial snapshot?

- How did you get to where you are now? What have you learned and overcome along the way?

- Have you made any mistakes that require grace and self-forgiveness?

- Is there someone who played a positive role in your financial journey that you could reach out to and thank?

- Is there someone who played a negative role in your situation that you need to forgive to move forward?

"A budget is telling
your money where to go
instead of wondering
where it went."

—John Maxwell

Chapter 4

MINDFUL SPENDING

One of my favorite Instagram reels shows a fighter jet performing a touch-and-go on an aircraft carrier. The jet's tires barely touch down before taking off again, with the caption "My paycheck entering my bank account."

Do you relate?

I sure do! Perhaps it's happened to you too—a paycheck comes in, you get excited, pay a couple bills, and suddenly it's all gone. By the end of the month, you find yourself wondering, **"Where did all the money go?"**

If that reel feels a little too real, you're not alone.

If you want to know where it's going, you'll need to start tracking it. Monitoring how you spend your money is a crucial step towards mastering your finances—a habit commonly known as budgeting.

Personally, I don't particularly care for the word "budget"—it feels too much like "diet." Both of these words evoke thoughts of restriction, self-denial, and shame. When we talk about reviewing our past spending, we'll refer to it as reviewing our spending. Different words = different feelings. When people talk about budgeting, they often mean, "Did you follow the money rules?" It's no wonder some people call it "the b-word"! But when approached through a lens of mindfulness, reviewing your spending becomes less about restriction and control and more about awareness and alignment.

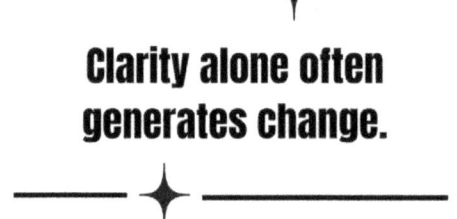

Clarity alone often generates change.

Author Barbara Stanny writes, "Clarity alone often generates change," and I have certainly found this to be true! The benefits of this clarity around spending can be quite impactful:

1. **You'll stop wasting money.** I'm not talking about cutting out avocado toast, lattes, or whatever the media is currently criticizing millennials for buying. I'm talking about money leaving your account without providing you any real value in return. This includes unused subscriptions you keep forgetting to cancel, duplicate payments, and paying for a higher level of service than you utilize.

   It can also mean identifying fraud on your accounts. According to FTC data, in 2023 alone, American consumers reported losing more than $10 billion to fraud. If you don't scan your transactions regularly, you might miss these things.

2. **You'll notice your patterns.** You may find you're spending more in certain areas than you realized. This spending may align with your values and fit within your cash flow. However, if it doesn't align with your values or exceeds your spending capacity, you'll want to shift your spending habits.

3. **You'll know your number.** Understanding how much you spend each month makes it easier to define and work towards financial goals, like having 3 to 6 months of expenses in savings.

To more easily identify and track patterns, you'll want to use a budgeting app that consolidates all your spending in one place. Most of these apps allow you to connect your checking, savings, and credit card accounts in real time, showing both your balances and transactions.

When your transactions are synced, you can assign them to categories like "groceries," "eating out," or "health and fitness." Most apps come with default budget categories, and some allow you to create categories as well.

When it comes to frequency, I find it works best to **review your spending at least weekly** to avoid falling behind. The more categorizing transactions becomes part of your routine, the easier it gets.

Money Patterns

As you review your spending, get curious, not critical, and give yourself grace. Look for patterns and meaning: are there stressors or emotions influencing your spending habits? Do you spend differently depending on who you're with or the time of the month or year? What values does your spending reflect?

As you observe your spending patterns, consider which align with your goals and values and which hold you back.

Patterns that are in alignment might include going on coffee dates with friends to nurture your relationships or paying for a gym membership that you actively use to stay in shape. Out-of-alignment patterns, on the other hand, might involve spending beyond your capacity or going shopping to avoid dealing with unpleasant feelings.

Some patterns may actually be tied to mental health diagnoses. For instance, if you struggle with depression or ADHD, spending might provide temporary relief by offering a dopamine boost. Similarly, individuals with bipolar disorder may experience spending spikes during manic phases.

My ADHD can impact my spending, especially when hyperfixations hit. I can go from never thinking about a hobby to needing all the supplies within an hour. Case in point: One December, I saw a pair of clay earrings on Pinterest and decided I'd make them as Christmas gifts to "save money." Within minutes, my Amazon cart was full of clay, cutters, and earring hooks. Thankfully, I've learned that my ADHD makes me impulsive with new hobbies, so I gave myself a 48-hour cooling-off period. When I was still excited two days later, I pared down my cart to just the basics. I made 40 pairs of earrings in a couple of days—then completely lost interest.

If you find your spending is impacted by a mental health condition, you may find it helpful to work with a therapist who has experience helping people with the condition you have. Even if they don't have a financial background, they can help you notice how your mental health impacts your spending and provide helpful tools.

Even without a mental health diagnosis, you might still struggle with compulsive or emotional spending. Here are a few questions to ask yourself to increase your mindfulness around spending:

- Why am I buying this?

- How am I hoping this purchase will make me feel?

- Am I trying to impress or gain approval from someone?

- Am I avoiding something?

Here are some strategies for managing impulse spending:

- Implement a waiting period for purchases over a certain amount. For example, wait 24 hours before buying anything over $100.

- When you add items to your Amazon cart, leave them there for a few days. Only finalize the purchase if it still feels important after the waiting period.

- Don't be afraid to return impulse purchases or anything you change your mind on!

- If certain apps make it too easy to spend mindlessly (again, looking at you Amazon!), consider deleting it from your phone.

Addressing Common Objections

I get it—no matter what we call it, you might still feel resistant to reviewing your spending. Let's tackle some of the most common objections head-on:

Objection #1: I want the freedom to spend my money how I want.

I hear you—no one likes feeling restricted, and freedom is important. But refusing to track your spending or stick to a plan because you don't want to feel limited is like planning an adventure and rejecting the idea of using a map.

A map is what gets you where you want to go.

- YOU pick the destination.
- YOU choose the route.
- YOU are in the driver's seat.

Planning and reviewing your spending is simply a way to ensure you're not wasting time and effort going in the wrong direction. True freedom comes from knowing your money is working for you, not against you.

Objection #2: I don't have the time.

It may take time upfront, but once you've connected your accounts and set up categories and automations in your budgeting app, you can put your budget on autopilot. It will save you time in the long run while keeping your finances on track.

Objection #3: I'm afraid of what I'll find.

This is a big one—fear of facing the truth about your spending can feel overwhelming. Maybe you're worried about uncovering mistakes or needing to make changes you're not ready for.

Remember, curiosity over criticism. Consider this your starting line for the next phase of your money journey. Even if you *have* made financial mistakes (which we all have), please don't beat yourself up over them. What matters now is that you do the hard thing so you can master your money.

Objection #4: I don't think it's necessary.

If you're able to pay your credit cards off and have money left in your account at the end of the month, it may feel like you don't need to track your spending. But what if you could have even more money left to invest and spend on things that truly matter to you?

Imagine traveling more or buying more plants or donating to causes you care about—imagine more money for what matters to you! Don't flush your hard-earned money down the toilet just because you can afford to. Taking the time to track your spending gives you the awareness you need to make sure your money is working for you. Isn't that worth the effort?

How Much Should I Be Spending?

I often get asked, "How much is normal to spend on (fill in the blank)?" My instinctive response to this question is that it doesn't matter what's "normal"— what matters is what makes sense for you and your situation. On the other hand, I also know it helps to have an idea of what others spend on things.

That being said, let's take a look at how two people with mostly similar financials have different spending capacity based on just a couple differences. Let's imagine they're roommates with the exact same income and bills, but one major difference—one of them graduated college with student loans and credit card debt.

DEBT-FREE BUDGET	IN-DEBT BUDGET

$50,000 Gross Salary, $3,500/month take home after paying 16% in taxes*

Rent and Utilities: $1,050 (30%)
Transportation: $350 (10%)
Insurance: $350 (10%)
Groceries: $350 (10%)
Health: $175 (5%)

Personal: $525 (15%)	**Personal: $225 (6%)**
Eating Out: $100	*Eating Out: $50*
Hair/Nails: $100	*Hair/Nails: $50*
Clothes: $125	*Clothes: $75*
Travel: $200	*Travel: $50*

Save/Invest: $350 (10%)	Student Loans: $500
Give: $350 (10%)	Personal Loan Payment: $300
(no debt payments)	Save/Invest: $100
	Give: $100

*theoretical tax rate including payroll taxes + federal and state income taxes

In this example, both individuals spend the same amount on rent, utilities, transportation, insurance, groceries, and health expenses. But because one of them has **$800** each month being eaten up by debt payments, that person has significantly less for personal spending. On paper it's just math; in real life it might look like that person turning down dinner invites, missing out on trips, and not being able to give, save, or invest as much as they'd like to. And if they look at how much their roommate is spending as what's "normal" and spend the same amount, they'll put themselves deeper into debt.

PRO TIP

Be extremely careful when comparing your financial situation with someone else's. You don't know who has more to spend than you because they received a family inheritance or bought a house because their parents gifted them a down payment. You also don't know who looks like they're a lot better off than you, but they're drowning in debt trying to maintain a lifestyle beyond what they can afford.

When it comes to how you're spending your money, your decisions need to be based on your situation.

CHAPTER WRAP-UP

Key Takeaways

- Speak about money in ways that feel positive, and use mindful spending to keep your finances aligned with your values.

- Clarity can prompt shifts in spending without creating rules.

- Mental health conditions often influence money behavior.

Key Actions

- Link your spending accounts to a budgeting app and review your spending each week.

- Write down the patterns that you observe when you review your spending.

- Reach out to a therapist, coach, or financial advisor to help you work through your spending patterns as they relate to your emotions and mental health.

Journal Prompt

- What comes to mind when you hear the word "budget"?

- Where did these feelings or beliefs originate, and how are they serving you?

- Do you currently know where your money is going? How does that make you feel?

- If you answered no to the question above, imagine what your life would be like if you did know where your money was going. How would it feel? What would change?

- Were you surprised by any patterns you observed? Did you feel encouraged or discouraged?

"Your greatest asset
is your earning ability."

—Brian Tracy

Chapter 5

UNDERSTANDING YOUR INCOME

Is Spending Less Really the Answer?

I'm pretty sure I'll always shop at thrift stores, no matter how much I earn. There's just something about the thrill of the hunt—that moment you score a "too good to be true" deal, like the perfect little black dress I recently found for $5, name brand and in flawless condition. I used to take pride in tallying up how much I'd "saved" by spending less, but lately I've started to look at it differently.

How much time and energy did I spend finding that deal? What if I had used that same effort to connect with a new client? What if, instead of focusing so much on cutting my spending, I focused on making more?

It's easy to pour our energy into cutting back—buying secondhand, making coffee at home, skipping the guac. And those choices can absolutely help. But what if you could have the guac *and* reach your goals faster by focusing on growing your income?

There's only so much you can cut. But your earning potential? That's unlimited. Grasping this truth early on in your career will have an exponential impact on your long-term financial success.

Choosing to Make More Money

I grew up with the mindset that your income was fixed, and that being good with money simply meant spending less than you made. I saw being "low income" as something to be adapted to, not something to be changed.

As a child eager to participate in extracurriculars like summer camps or dance classes, I learned to seek out scholarships for low-income families. I also learned to barter for things I couldn't afford, like the time I cleaned a photographer's home in exchange for my senior photos.

Growing up this way led me to internalize the idea that I was inherently low-income. I didn't see myself as a person who currently earned less, but instead saw "low-income" as a defining aspect of my identity. No matter how hard I worked, I consistently earned less than those around me, and instead of questioning why I simply accepted it. I was a perfect example of what author Barbara Stanny refers to in her *book Overcoming Underearning* as an "underearner."

Stanny describes underearners as follows: "Under earners can be terrible snobs. They're ambivalent or downright negative about money and/or people who have it. They dislike the wealthy, take great pride in living on a shoestring, believe there is virtue in being poor, and criticize those too focused on their finances."

I didn't see myself as a victim—more like a martyr. I chose to sacrifice my potential to earn a really great living for my family, and I felt noble for doing so. For me, the hardest part of making more money wasn't about doing the things that would increase my income, though those were also hard. The hardest part was recognizing how I had clung to this false sense of pride—and letting it go.

The glass ceiling at work is nothing compared to the lead ceiling in my head.

As one of Stanny's friends says in her book *Secrets of Six-Figure Women*: "The glass ceiling at work is nothing compared to the lead ceiling in my head."

Breaking Through Your Financial Comfort Zone

What determines the limit of our earning ability? Is it shaped by the family we're born into? The place we live and the level of education that we achieve? Or is it defined by talent, intelligence, and hard work?

The truth is, when it comes to how much money we think we can (or should) make, we tend to stay within a financial comfort zone. Most people don't realize that this zone exists or that it varies person to person. We likely surround ourselves with friends and family who share a similar financial comfort zone, reinforcing our perception of what "normal" looks like.

For someone from a wealthier family, "normal" might include buying expensive clothes, attending private schools, and traveling internationally. In contrast, someone from a less wealthy household might see "normal" as buying clothes at thrift stores, only joining sports or programs when scholarships are available, and limiting travel to car camping or visiting family.

Rick Kahler, a Certified Financial Therapist, explains: "The expectations people grow up with tend to keep them in their financial comfort zones. These zones are artificial financial boundaries that we impose on ourselves, and they are not necessarily defined by what we can or cannot afford. Yet we become uncomfortable if we move too far outside them."

When we approach the low end of our financial comfort zone, it feels like we aren't earning enough. Naturally, we tend to take action to restore a standard of living that feels "normal" to us.

What's less obvious is how we respond when we approach the upper end of that range. Theoretically, we'd all lean into making more money. But in reality, many of us actually start to subconsciously rein ourselves in to stay within our financial comfort zone.

We might get complacent and stop taking steps to advance in our careers. Perhaps we procrastinate on important tasks that would move us forward and then claim we don't have time. Or maybe we're just not trying for bigger things. Maybe we're not applying for that great job or asking for that raise. Whatever the reason (aka. excuse), deep down we've decided we're making enough money and have taken our foot off the gas.

To be clear, if you are completely content with your income and how it supports your life, I'm not trying to disrupt that. I don't want to create discontent or encourage a never-ending pursuit of more. Instead, I want you to reflect: are you genuinely content with your current income?

Does it actually support your ideal life, or is it simply a number you've internalized as "good enough"?

Defining Your Ideal Income

When defining your ideal income, it can be helpful to shift your focus from the dollar amount to what those dollars will allow you to achieve. This will become your "why" as you step out of your financial comfort zone and work toward your ideal income—and your ideal life.

Here are a few examples of goals and values I want my income to support:

- Buying clothes that make me feel confident and comfortable.

- Taking my family somewhere sunny every winter.

- Paying off my credit cards in full each month.

- Helping my kids graduate from college debt-free.

- Maintaining my current lifestyle in retirement.

Gender

Let's talk briefly about gender and income. A quick Google search for "women and income" will mostly return results about the gender pay gap. According to Pew Research's 2022 study, women, on average, still earn $0.82 for every dollar earned by men—a slight increase from $0.80 in 2002. The gender pay gap is real, unfair, and worthy of continued advocacy. **But if you focus solely on closing it, you risk overlooking what you can control—how you manage your own money.** Don't tie your financial success to a needle that has barely moved in two decades. In this book, we are focused on moving the needle in areas we can control, which in this chapter looks like understanding how much we're currently earning.

Reading Your Paystub

Want to know how much you actually make? Start by reading your paystub. It shows how much your employer is paying you, what's being withheld for taxes, and what's being deducted for things like 401(k) contributions and health insurance. Here are the things to look at when reviewing your paystub to better understand your income:

Pay Period

If your pay period range is 14 days, you are paid bi-weekly, meaning you get paid every other week and will have 26 pay periods per year. To calculate your annual income, multiply your paycheck amount by 26.

If your pay period range is 15 days or more (except for February), you are paid bi-monthly, resulting in 24 pay periods per year. In this case, multiply your paycheck amount by 24 to determine your annual income.

Gross Income

Your gross income is your paycheck amount before any deductions. It should match the salary or hourly rate you agreed upon. Double-check that your hours are being calculated correctly and that any negotiated raises are accurately reflected.

UNDERSTANDING YOUR INCOME

Federal Income Tax

Federal income tax works on a tiered system with different tax brackets, as well as various credits and deductions. If you're an employee, your employer withholds federal taxes from your paycheck and sends them to the IRS on your behalf. The amount they withhold is based on the information you provide on your W-4 form when you start a job. (W-4 stands for *Employee's Withholding Certificate*—not to be confused with your W-2, which shows how much you earned and paid in taxes each year.)

The W-4 helps estimate how much income tax to withhold, but it's not an exact science. Tax calculations vary based on your income, deductions, credits, and even your state's tax rules. If too much is withheld, you'll get a refund—but that's not a bonus, it's money you overpaid. If too little is withheld, you'll owe the IRS when you file your tax return.

If you consistently receive a large refund or owe a big tax bill each year, it might be time to update your W-4 to better match your actual tax situation.

State Income Tax

Some states charge income tax in addition to federal taxes. While a few states use your federal W-4 to determine how much to withhold, most have their own state-specific withholding form. States also vary in how they tax income: some have a **flat tax**, where all income is taxed at the same rate, while others use a **tiered system** similar to federal tax brackets.

In most cases, you owe state income tax based on where you live. However, if you **commute across state lines** or **earn income in another state**, you might also owe taxes there—though many states offer credits to prevent double taxation.

Understanding how income taxes differ from state to state helps you plan ahead, avoid surprises, and get a clearer picture of your **true take-home pay**—especially if you're comparing job opportunities in different states.

Credits v Deductions

Keep in mind that **tax credits and deductions aren't the same**. Tax **credits** reduce your tax bill *dollar for dollar*—a $1,000 credit lowers your taxes by $1,000. **Deductions**, on the other hand, reduce your **taxable income**. If you're in the 22% tax bracket, a $1,000 deduction would save you $220 in taxes. In short, **credits are more valuable** because they directly lower what you owe, not just the amount you're taxed on.

CREDITS V. DEDUCTIONS

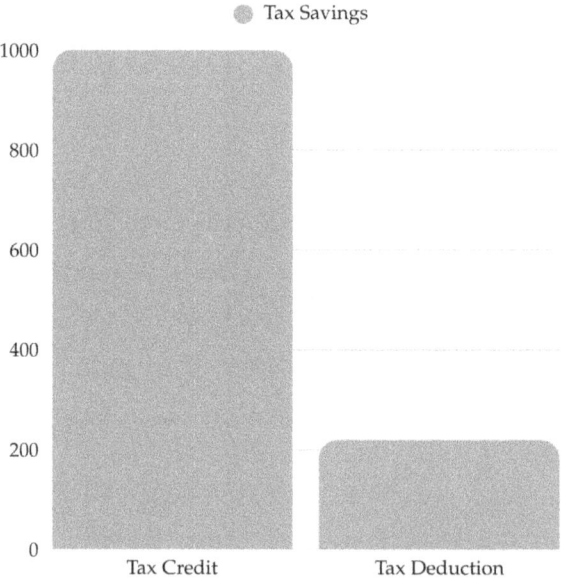

this example uses a hypothetical tax rate of 22%

Tax Brackets

Another important thing to understand about taxes is that the tax brackets are tiered—each portion of your income is taxed at a different rate. It's a common misconception that once your income crosses a threshold, your entire income gets taxed at that higher rate, but that's not how it works.

"This isn't a tax prep guide, and you don't need to memorize brackets. What matters is getting the big picture so you understand why your take-home pay looks different from your gross salary."

See the following visual depiction of how tax brackets actually work.

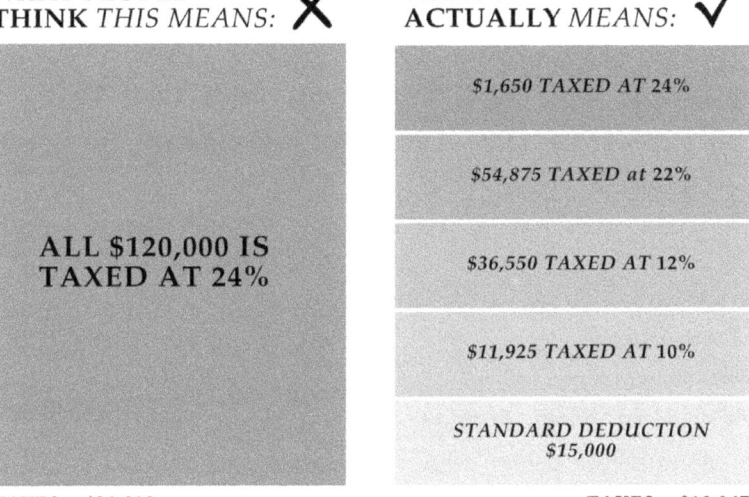

"I'M MAKING $120,000 SO I'M IN THE 24% TAX BRACKET."

WHAT PEOPLE **THINK** *THIS MEANS:* ✗   *WHAT IT* **ACTUALLY** *MEANS:* ✓

WHAT PEOPLE THINK	WHAT IT ACTUALLY MEANS
ALL $120,000 IS TAXED AT 24%	$1,650 TAXED AT 24%
	$54,875 TAXED at 22%
	$36,550 TAXED AT 12%
	$11,925 TAXED AT 10%
	STANDARD DEDUCTION $15,000
TAXES = $28,800	*TAXES = $18,047*

*example showing only federal taxes for a single tax payer in 2025 without credits or deductions, besides the standard deduction

Payroll Taxes: Social Security and Medicare (FICA)

Social Security Tax

The Social Security portion of FICA is a federal payroll tax that funds retirement, disability, and survivor benefits. It's based on your gross wages before pre-tax deductions like 401(k) contributions or health insurance premiums. If you're a **W-2 employee**, your employer pays half, and the other half is withheld from your paycheck. If you're **self-employed**, you pay the full amount yourself through the self-employment tax.

Medicare Tax

The Medicare portion of FICA helps fund healthcare for people age 65 and older, as well as certain individuals with disabilities. Like Social Security, **W-2 employees** split the tax with their employer. **Self-employed workers** pay both halves.

Together, Social Security and Medicare taxes total **15.3%** for self-employed individuals and **7.65%** for employees (with employers covering the other 7.65%).

Other Deductions

This section of your paystub shows your contributions to your workplace retirement plan, Health Savings Account (HSA), and insurance premiums.

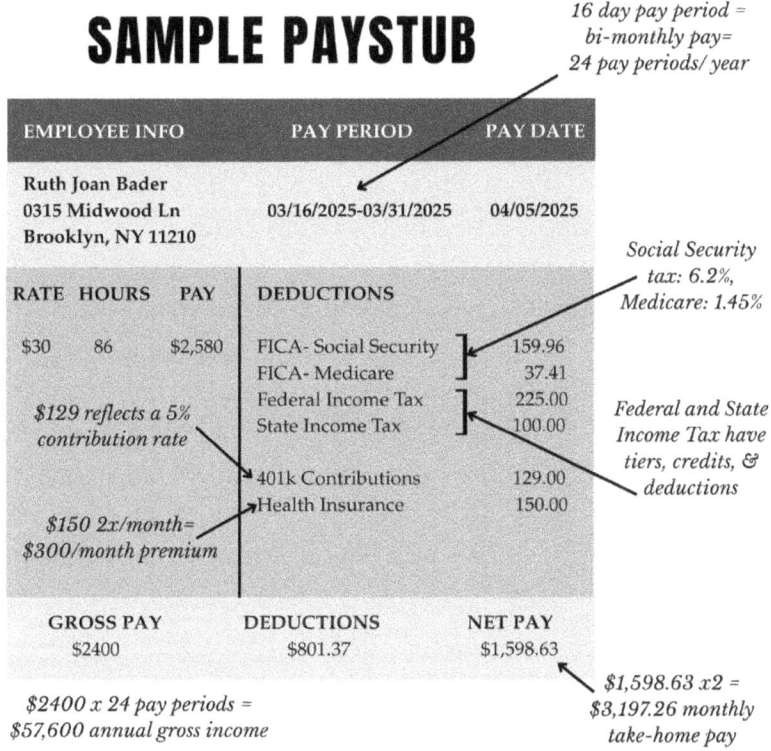

SAMPLE PAYSTUB

*16 day pay period =
bi-monthly pay=
24 pay periods/ year*

EMPLOYEE INFO	PAY PERIOD	PAY DATE
Ruth Joan Bader 0315 Midwood Ln Brooklyn, NY 11210	03/16/2025-03/31/2025	04/05/2025

*Social Security
tax: 6.2%,
Medicare: 1.45%*

RATE	HOURS	PAY	DEDUCTIONS	
$30	86	$2,580	FICA- Social Security	159.96
			FICA- Medicare	37.41
			Federal Income Tax	225.00
			State Income Tax	100.00
			401k Contributions	129.00
			Health Insurance	150.00

*$129 reflects a 5%
contribution rate*

*Federal and State
Income Tax have
tiers, credits, &
deductions*

*$150 2x/month=
$300/month premium*

GROSS PAY	DEDUCTIONS	NET PAY
$2400	$801.37	$1,598.63

*$2400 x 24 pay periods =
$57,600 annual gross income*

*$1,598.63 x2 =
$3,197.26 monthly
take-home pay*

Gross v Net: Understanding the Difference

There is often a significant difference between your gross income—the total amount earned before deductions—and net income, which is the amount deposited into your bank account. We tend to mentally anchor our earnings to our gross annual salary but experience our earnings as the net amount we take home. I've heard people say, "I'm making the most money I've ever made, but it doesn't feel like I'm making any more than I was before."

It can be frustrating when you negotiate a raise or secure a higher-paying salary then barely notice a difference in your spending power.

Understanding your take-home pay can transform how you perceive both the value of your time and your money.

Comparing Job Offers: It's More Than Just Salary

When evaluating a job offer or deciding between two jobs, don't focus only on the salary. Your total compensation includes much more than your paycheck. Here are key factors to consider:

- **401(k) match** – A strong match can add thousands to your retirement savings.

- **Health insurance** – Look at premiums, deductibles, copays, and out-of-pocket maximums. A lower salary with better insurance might actually leave you with more take-home income.

- **Paid time off (PTO)** – Vacation, sick leave, and holidays all matter, especially if work-life balance is a priority.

- **Flexibility** – Remote work options, flexible hours, or a shorter commute can greatly impact your quality of life.

- **Cost of living** – Where you live affects how far your salary goes. A $70,000 salary in a small town may go further than $90,000 in a high-cost city.

- **Other perks** – Think wellness programs, professional development support, bonuses, childcare assistance, or even commuter benefits.

Take time to weigh the full picture, not just the paycheck. A job with a slightly lower salary could be more valuable overall when you factor in benefits, lifestyle, and long-term financial growth.

CHAPTER WRAP-UP

Key Takeaways

- Your earning ability is your greatest financial asset. Spending less can help, but there's a limit to how much you can cut.

- Your mindset around money shapes your income, so recognize how internalized beliefs are subconsciously limiting your earning potential.

- Gross income isn't the same as take-home pay. Know the difference—and pay attention to what's being withheld or taxed.

- Pay goes beyond your hourly rate or salary. It includes benefits, remote work arrangements, time off, and professional development opportunities.

Key Actions

- Review your paystub, check for errors, consult HR if you have questions.

- Calculate your take-home pay to help with your budgeting and planning.

- Learn about the benefits your employer offers, including 401(k) match, insurance options, HSA/FSA access, PTO, and any other perks.

- If you receive a large tax refund or tax bill each year, consider adjusting your tax withholding.

Journal Prompts

- What kind of income did your family earn when you were growing up, and how did it shape your perspective on money?

- How does your current income level affect your lifestyle and goals?

- In what ways would your life change if your income increased?

- What income level would truly support the life you want? Go beyond just "getting by"—what income would allow you to live with freedom?

"The time to save for the future is now. Thanks to compounding interest, the earlier you start putting money away for the future, the more you will save."

—Alexa von Tobel

Chapter 6

RETIREMENT

How Does Retirement Work?

In a nutshell, retiring is when you stop working and earning a paycheck and transition to living on other income sources. These income sources can include investment accounts (such as a 401(k) or a Roth IRA), Social Security, pensions, or rental properties.

There are entire books written on retirement planning, Social Security filing strategies, etc. For the sake of this book, we're focusing more on how to get started on saving for retirement, not necessarily going in depth on strategies or how to create a concise financial plan for retirement.

Investing vs. Intentional Spending

Here I define investing as putting your money into something that generates more money. Investments create returns in two ways: by providing immediate income or by appreciating in value, enabling you to make a profit when you sell.

This is different from when you spend your money on things like healthy food, gym memberships, therapy, and similar expenses. You may hear people describe these expenses as "making an investment in yourself." While these expenses may provide benefits such as improved health and a higher quality of life, they don't generate income. Instead of calling these categories investments, we'll use the term **intentional spending**.

I often see people look at investing and intentional spending as competing priorities. For example, someone who values travel might choose to spend their money on trips instead of saving for retirement. But they're not simply choosing travel over an arbitrary savings goal—they're prioritizing travel now at the expense of being able to travel later. Investing means setting aside money today so you can maintain your spending habits in the future.

Keep in mind it's not an either/or choice—it's about finding a balance between immediate gratification and caring for your future self. Consider eating out as an example: If you spend a few hundred dollars each month on dining and want to ensure you can continue enjoying restaurants and coffee dates in retirement, investing just $100 per month with an average annual return of 8% over 30 years could grow to $149,000!

Cheryl's Story

Cheryl struggled to find money to invest. She rarely spent much on herself but regularly contributed to several causes she deeply cared about.

The idea of investing money for her own future, rather than supporting organizations doing important work, felt selfish to her. With a roof over her head and food to eat, she questioned why she should keep anything more for herself.

I deeply admire Cheryl's heart for helping others and how her compassion drives her to selfless action. However, I could also see what would happen to her ability to give if she didn't find a way to save for her future. So I asked her, "Cheryl, do you only want to help these causes now, or do you want to be able to continue giving when you retire?"

"Well, I want to keep giving, of course," she replied.

"Where will you get the money to do that?" I asked her.

"I hadn't really thought about that," she admitted.

During our conversation, Cheryl began to realize that if she didn't start putting away money now, she wouldn't have anything to give later.

How Much Do I Need to Retire?

One of the most common questions I hear is, "How much do I need to retire?" People want to know the number they need to have in their investments so they can stop working and not worry about running out of money. The truth is, there's no single "magic number," because retirement income usually comes from more than one source and depends on how much monthly income each person needs. For most people, part of their income will come from fixed sources like Social Security or a pension. The rest will need to come from their savings and investments.

So instead of asking, "How much do I need total?" a better question is, **"How much income do I need my investments to produce?"**

Let's break it down with an example. Imagine two people, both of whom receive $2,500 a month from Social Security. The difference is that one of them needs $4,000 a month to live on, and the other needs $5,000. The first person will need $1,500 per month from their investments, while the second person needs $2,500 per month from their investments.

Using a 4% withdrawal rate (the amount you take from your investments each year as a percentage) from their retirement savings, that means the first person would need about **$450,000** in investments and the second would need around **$750,000**. This is why the work you do in understanding your income has such a big impact on your retirement planning! Let's look at the numbers side by side:

HOW MUCH DO I NEED TO RETIRE?

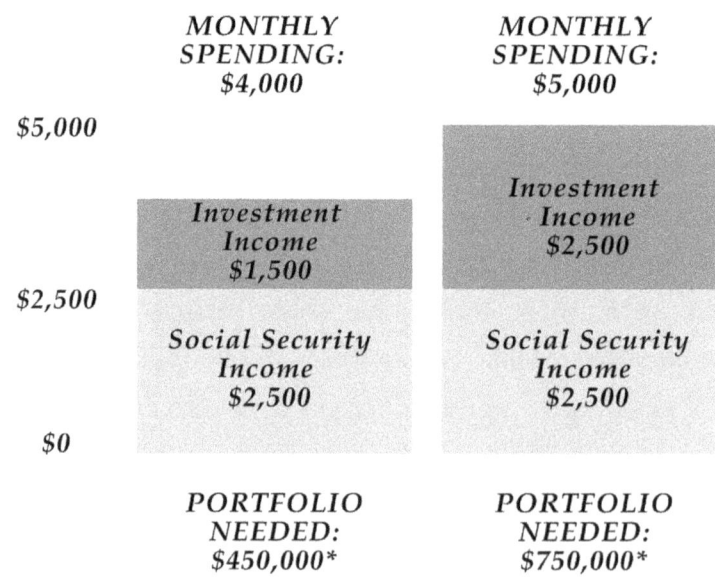

	MONTHLY SPENDING: $4,000	MONTHLY SPENDING: $5,000
$5,000		
		Investment Income $2,500
	Investment Income $1,500	
$2,500		
	Social Security Income $2,500	Social Security Income $2,500
$0		
	PORTFOLIO NEEDED: $450,000*	PORTFOLIO NEEDED: $750,000*

based on a 4% withdrawal rate

Investment Accounts

You know that feeling when you run into someone you've spoken with multiple times and you know you should remember their name—but you can't, and now it feels too late to ask? Talking about retirement accounts and investments can feel the same way. You might think, "I'm old enough, successful enough—I should know what a Roth is and how a 401(k) works, right?"

If this sounds familiar, let me assure you—you are not alone! I've worked with countless people of all ages across industries like real estate, insurance, and management. At some point in our conversations, they often say, "I feel like I should know this by now, but . . ." Unfortunately, the embarrassment of not knowing something often prevents people from asking the questions they need to.

I'm not going to make you ask. I'll assume that you may not know the names of any investment accounts, and I'll introduce them to you one at a time—just like that friend at a party that asks someone's name for you so you don't have to admit you already forgot it.

How to Save for Retirement

There are two main ways to fund a retirement account. The first is through your employer. These accounts—like a 401(k) or 403(b)—are typically funded by automatic payroll deductions, and in some cases your employer may also contribute. The second option is to open your own Individual Retirement Account (IRA) or Roth IRA. You can fund it by rolling over money from a previous employer's plan or by making direct contributions from your own income.

In the next section, we'll take a closer look at the most common types of retirement accounts—how they work, how they're taxed, and how to decide which ones might be right for you.

401(k)

The 401(k) is the most common type of retirement plan and is typically offered by employers as a benefit. A 401(k) is considered an "employer-sponsored" retirement plan, meaning your employer sets it up and handles contributions by deducting money from your paycheck. Many plans also offer a company match, which is essentially "free money." Don't leave it on the table!

Here are a few terms to help you better understand how 401(k)s work:

- **Company match**

  The employer matches your contributions up to a certain amount.

  Example 1: A 100% match up to 4% of your salary. If your gross income is $5,000 per month, you'd contribute $200 (4% of $5,000), and your employer contributes $200.

  Example 2: A 50% match up to 4%. You'd contribute $200, and your employer would contribute $100 (50% of your $200).

- **Full match**

  This is the amount you need to contribute to receive the entire company match. In both examples above, contributing 4% of your pay gets you the full match.

- **Maxing out**

  This means contributing the maximum amount the IRS allows in a year. For 2025, that limit is $23,500 (not including any employer contributions).

- **Vesting**

  Some plans have vesting schedules, meaning you need to stay at the company for a certain period before employer contributions fully belong to you. This only applies to the match, not the money you contribute.

  - **Graded vesting:** You gradually "earn" the match over time (for example, 25% per year). If your plan vests at 25% per year and you leave the company after two years, you would get to keep 50% of what the employer contributed on your behalf.

  - **Cliff vesting:** You get 0% until you reach a milestone (often 3 years), then 100% of the employer contribution is yours. If you leave anytime before that milestone, you forfeit what the employer contributed.

  - **Timing:** Note that the vesting schedule is based on your time with the company, not how long the account is open. Leaving it open a while longer after you've left won't help you keep any more of the match.

Traditional vs. Roth 401(k)

Most plans let you choose between Traditional (pretax) and Roth (after-tax) contributions.

- Traditional is often best for higher earners looking to reduce their current tax bill.

- Roth is great if you're in a lower tax bracket now and want tax-free income in retirement.

Tip: If you opt for Roth contributions, adjust your tax withholdings—these contributions don't reduce your taxable income like Traditional contributions.

TRADITIONAL	ROTH
Tax Break Now	Tax Free Later
Withdrawals Subject to Tax + Penalty Before Age 59 1/2	Contributions Accessible Tax + Penalty Free at any age
Withdrawals Subject to Unknown Future Tax Rates	Taxes have already been paid at current Tax Rates
Contribution AND Earnings Taxed at Withdrawal	Earnings Never Taxed if Withdrawn After age 59 1/2

SIMPLE IRA

Another common type of retirement plan is a SIMPLE IRA. SIMPLE IRAs typically offer a 3% match with no vesting schedule, meaning your employer's contributions are yours immediately, regardless of how long you work there.

SEP IRA

A SEP IRA, short for Simplified Employee Pension, is a retirement plan commonly used by self-employed individuals. This plan may allow those with self-employment income to contribute significantly more than they could to an Individual IRA. The maximum contribution is calculated as a percentage of business income, up to an IRS limit.

Individual IRAs

There are two ways to establish an IRA, whether Traditional or Roth: you can either set one up from scratch by making contributions from your bank account or roll over an old 401(k) or another retirement plan from a former employer.

Traditional

Contributions to a Traditional IRA are tax-deductible, and the money grows tax-deferred, meaning you won't owe taxes on the account's growth or earnings until withdrawal. However, in exchange for this tax break, 100% of your withdrawals—both contributions and earnings—will be taxable when you take them out.

Pros

- Tax deduction now

- Tax-deferred growth and earnings

- Save for retirement even if your work doesn't offer a 401(k)

- Flexibility around when and how you contribute

- Control over what company you use as your investment provider

Cons

- Future withdrawals are fully taxable at a not-yet-known tax rate

- Early withdrawals (before age 59 1/2) incur a 10% "premature distribution" IRS penalty

- Low contribution limit compared to 401(k), SIMPLE IRA, and similar employer plans

PRO TIP

There are income limitations to being able to deduct your contributions to a Traditional IRA, depending on your income and whether you and/or your spouse have access to a retirement plan through work.

TRADITIONAL

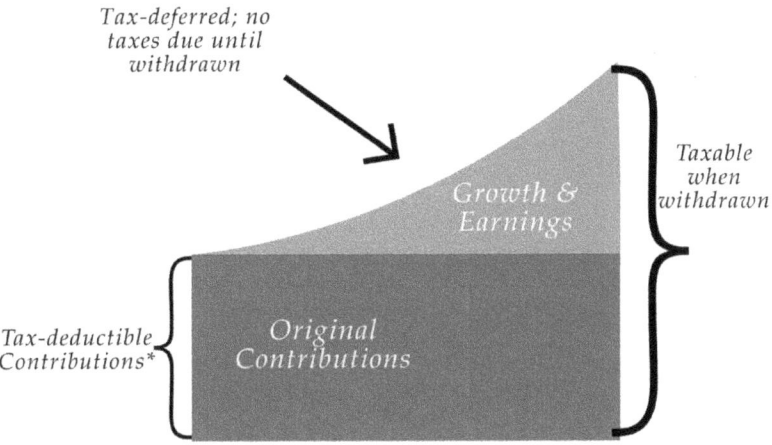

Tax-deferred; no taxes due until withdrawn

Growth & Earnings

Taxable when withdrawn

*Tax-deductible Contributions**

Original Contributions

*it is possible to make non-deductible contributions, this is part of an advanced strategy not covered in this book

Roth IRA

Contributions to a Roth IRA are not deductible, but they grow tax-free. This means you'll never pay taxes on the account's growth or earnings (I call this magic!). And on top of that, you can access your Roth contributions penalty-free at any time.

Be sure to note that if you withdraw more than your contributions and dip into the growth in your account, that portion of your withdrawal will be taxed and penalized if you are under age 59 ½. For example, if you invest $5,000 in a Roth and it grows to $8,000, then you pull it all out, you will owe tax and penalty on the $3,000 of growth in the account.

Roth IRAs also limit what you can contribute, based on your income. Unlike Traditional IRAs, it doesn't matter if you're eligible for a retirement plan through work.

ROTH

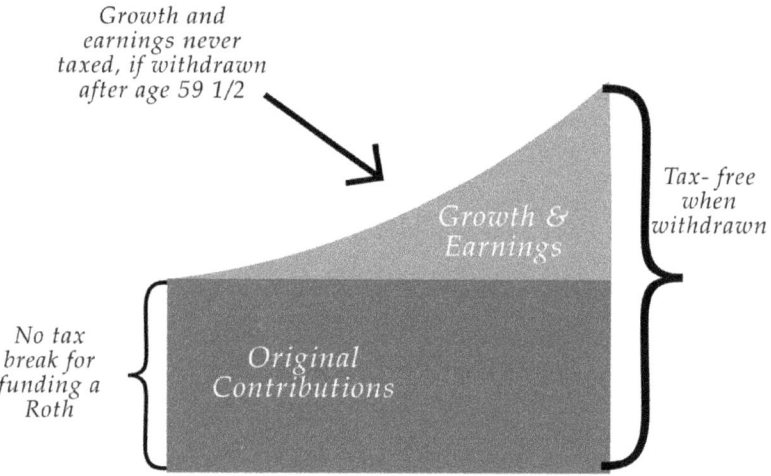

Growth and earnings never taxed, if withdrawn after age 59 1/2

Tax- free when withdrawn

Growth & Earnings

No tax break for funding a Roth

Original Contributions

The Power of Compound Interest

Compound interest is one of the most powerful forces in personal finance. It's what happens when you earn interest not just on your original investment but also on the interest that money has already earned. Over time, this creates a snowball effect—your savings grow faster and faster the longer they're invested.

Of course, compound interest can also work *against* you—like with credit card debt, where unpaid interest gets added to your balance and starts racking up interest of its own. But when you're investing for retirement, compound interest is your best friend. And one of the most important advantages is something totally within your control: **when you start**.

Let's say you and a coworker are both getting serious about retirement savings. You decide to start at age 30, while your coworker starts at 50. You both contribute $500 a month and earn an average annual return of 8%. By the time you reach age 65, you'll have just over **$1.2 million** saved—while your coworker will have a little over **$340,000**. The difference? Time! Here's the bottom line:

1. Compound interest works best the longer you give it to grow.

2. You want it working for you (through investing) not against you (through debt).

3. Even small amounts, started early, can lead to massive results.

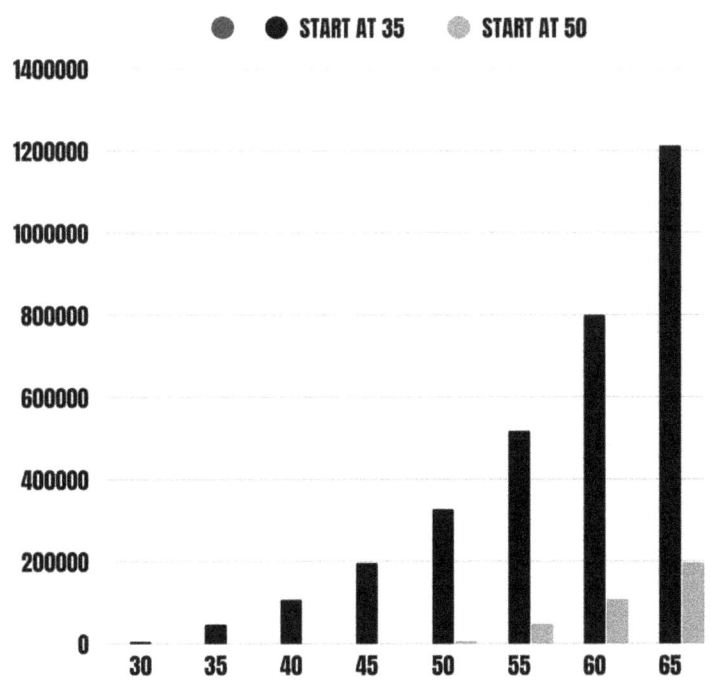

START AT 35   START AT 50

Nonretirement Accounts

We've talked about retirement accounts—their features, tax benefits, and contribution limits—but you're not limited to those. You can also invest in nonretirement accounts, often called **nonqualified** or **taxable investment accounts**. These accounts can hold stocks, bonds, mutual funds, index funds, ETFs, etc. They don't have contribution limits, income restrictions, or early withdrawal penalties. You can use the money for anything: a car, a home renovation, your child's college expenses, or even to fund early retirement before age 59 1/2.

Because these accounts don't come with tax breaks on the front end or back end, it's important to be mindful of the tax consequences. When you sell an investment for more than you paid, you'll owe **capital gains** tax on the difference. I don't want to get too technical here, but just know that if you make money in the stock market, you'll want to make sure you're aware of what taxes you will owe so you can plan ahead.

With some planning and strategy, nonqualified investment accounts can offer flexibility and help you grow wealth beyond retirement.

Social Security

You might be decades away from collecting Social Security, but it will likely play a significant role in your retirement income someday. So it's worth having a basic understanding of how it works—and hey, it might even give you something interesting to bring up next time you're chatting with your parents.

Social Security was created in 1935 when President Franklin D. Roosevelt signed the Social Security Act into law. The goal? To provide retirement income for Americans aged 65 and older. The program is funded by payroll taxes—you pay half and your employer pays the other half. You become eligible after earning at least 40 "credits," which typically means about ten years of work. There are also spousal and survivor benefits available in certain situations.

The age you start collecting Social Security has a big impact on how much you receive. You can start as early as age 62, but your benefit will be permanently reduced. Your "full retirement age" (FRA) is 67 if you were born in 1960 or later. If you start before then, there's also an earnings limit: For every $2 you earn above the threshold, $1 is temporarily withheld from your benefit. Once you reach your FRA, that earnings limit disappears—you can earn as much as you want without any reduction in your monthly check.

If you wait beyond full retirement age, your benefit grows by about 8% per year until age 70. After that, it stops increasing. Here's an example: if your benefit at age 67 is **$2,200** per month, at 62, you'd receive about **$1,500**, and at age 70, you'd receive around **$2,770** per month. And those payments last for life!

You may also hear concerns about Social Security "running out of money." While the trust fund that helps support benefits may be depleted in the future, it's unlikely that the program will disappear altogether. More likely, the government will make changes, such as raising the full retirement age or adjusting benefit formulas, to keep it going. In other words, your benefit may be reduced but is unlikely to actually "go away."

Pension

Does it seem like pensions are a relic from the past? In many ways, they are. Traditional pensions have become increasingly rare in the private sector, but they're still alive and well in certain fields. If you work in public service—like teaching, government, law enforcement, or firefighting—there's a good chance a pension is part of your benefits package. Some union jobs in industries like transportation or manufacturing still offer them too. If you're one of the lucky ones who has access to a pension, it's worth understanding how it works—because the fine print can make a big difference in your future.

Most pensions are what's called **"defined benefit" plans**, which means they guarantee you a set monthly income in retirement based on your salary and how long you've worked. The longer you stay, the more **service credit** you earn. Just note that part-time work usually earns partial credit—so if you work half-time for 10 years, you'll likely end up with about **5 years of service credit**.

Some systems add in a "defined contribution" component—more like a 401(k)—where you and/or your employer contribute regularly and the account grows over time. A few plans are hybrids and blend both approaches. When weighing your options, ask yourself:

- Do I plan to stay long enough to vest and receive the benefit?

- Do I want the stability of guaranteed income or the flexibility to manage my own investments?

- What happens if I leave early or switch employers?

Pensions can be a huge asset—but they can also be confusing. The rules vary widely, and small choices can have lasting effects. If you're not sure, this is one of those moments when getting personalized advice is absolutely worth it.

CHAPTER WRAP-UP

Key Takeaways

- If you haven't already, start investing today. Set up monthly contributions and increase them as you're able.

- Saving part of your income for retirement allows you to continue spending on what's important to you when you're no longer earning a paycheck.

- A successful retirement depends not only on the amount of money you've saved but also on factors like your sources of income and your monthly living expenses.

Key Action Items

- Sign up for your 401(k) or another retirement plan offered through work.

- Increase your contribution if you're already signed up.

- If you don't have a 401(k) or want to invest more, set up an IRA or Roth IRA. Check the current income limits to ensure you're eligible to contribute.

Journal Prompts

- Imagine your life 20, 30, 40 years from now. How will you spend your days? Will you be traveling, eating out, attending concerts? Will you be helping out any friends of family members? Paint a picture of what you want your life to look like.

- Imagine you can have a conversation with your future self. What do you think she would tell you? Would she say thank you for setting her up for a good life?

Chapter 7

DEBT

My Debt Story

My early views on debt were shaped by Dave Ramsey, a man who has built a business empire teaching his anti-debt philosophy. He advocates that any kind of debt (other than a primary mortgage) is bad—including car loans, student loans, and even financing for investment properties. I believed in his program, followed it, and even taught it. It didn't just influence my financial philosophy—it was its foundation. Being debt-free was a core part of my identity and self-worth. It gave me a sense of control and, if I'm honest, a bit of a moral high ground. In a world that felt financially overwhelming, it was reassuring to believe I was doing the "right" thing—even if that sometimes meant judging myself (and others) a little too harshly.

I was determined to get through college without student loans. I attended a community college near home, taking one class at a time so I could work full-time and pay tuition out of pocket. I even took a year off when I moved to a new state to qualify for in-state tuition. I juggled multiple jobs, stretched every dollar, and accepted every bit of financial aid I could find. On paper, it looked like discipline and hustle—but underneath, it was also exhausting. And yet . . . it wasn't enough.

Eventually, I had to choose: take on student loans or drop out. I considered stepping away again to save up, but I was already years behind my peers. Most of my friends had graduated and started careers, while I was still cobbling together credits and crossing my fingers that my car wouldn't break down. I even thought about enrolling in a cheaper, less reputable online program—something I knew might hurt my chances of landing the kind of job I was aiming for.

So I made the choice that felt like a betrayal of everything I'd believed in: I borrowed student loans. I still remember the pit in my stomach when I signed the paperwork. I felt like I was doing something wrong—even though I'd done the math, weighed the options, and knew it was the smartest path forward.

Looking back, I have no regrets. But I *do* wish someone with financial experience had helped me navigate that decision without shame or fear. Someone who could say, "Yes, you're doing your best. And yes, this is still a financially sound move." Now I want to be that person for you.

In this chapter, I'll walk you through the ABCs of debt—the different types, how they work, and how to use debt wisely as a tool rather than a trap. I'll also help you build a plan to manage and pay off the debt you have—on your terms.

ABC's of Debt

When Is Debt a Good Idea

Keep in mind that not all debt is bad—sometimes it's necessary. You might have student debt that enabled you to pursue your dream job or increase your income. Perhaps you have credit card debt from car repairs that kept your vehicle running or expenses related to leaving a bad living situation. Maybe you incurred debt from a side gig that didn't pan out. Or you might even have some "dumb" debt from overspending or forgetting to cancel subscriptions.

Debt can be a tool to help you achieve your goals, but it can also be a trap that prevents you from reaching them. How do you decide whether it's a tool or a trap? It often comes down to the trade-off between risk and reward and whether you can comfortably afford the payments.

> **Debt can be a tool to help you achieve your goals, but it can also be a trap that prevents you from reaching them.**

Some types of debt, like payday loans, are almost always a trap. However, for most other types of debt, whether it's a tool or a trap depends on your unique situation and personal goals.

Let's talk a little about how debt works before we move on to some common types of loans.

Secured v Unsecured: What You Should Know

One important distinction when evaluating debt is whether it's **secured** or **unsecured**. Understanding the difference can help you make more confident, informed choices about debt.

Secured debt is backed by an asset the lender can take if you don't repay the loan. Common examples include mortgages and car loans. Because the lender has something to fall back on, these loans often come with lower interest rates and higher borrowing limits. **Secured credit cards** also fall into this category. They require a cash deposit that serves as collateral and are often used by people with little or no credit history to build a positive credit profile. While they tend to have **lower limits** and **higher interest rates**, they can be a useful stepping stone when you're getting started.

Unsecured debt, on the other hand, isn't tied to any specific asset. This includes credit cards, student loans, and medical bills. Because there's no collateral involved, lenders take on more risk—and usually charge **higher interest rates** or have **stricter approval requirements** as a result. Medical debt is a bit of an outlier. It's technically unsecured, but it usually doesn't accrue interest when you're on a payment plan through the provider. However, if left unpaid, it can be sent to collections—where fees and credit damage can still create long-term consequences.

Bottom line? Knowing the difference between secured and unsecured debt isn't just a vocabulary lesson—it's a key part of making debt work *for* you, not against you.

Understanding Your Credit Score

Your credit score is a measure of how reliable you are at managing your debt, not how good you are at managing your money. A more accurate name would be "debt management score." It's an unfortunate system that requires you to use debt to qualify for good terms on future loans, but it's the world we live in.

With limited exceptions, your credit score will determine what loans you get approved for and what interest rates you get. Depending on your situation, your credit score could cost or save you hundreds, thousands, even tens of thousands of dollars. It is essential to be mindful of your score long before you need to rely on it.

FICO is the most widely used credit score, often used by lenders to determine how likely you are to repay what you borrow. Scores range from 300 to 850, and they're calculated based on five main categories. Here's what goes into your score:

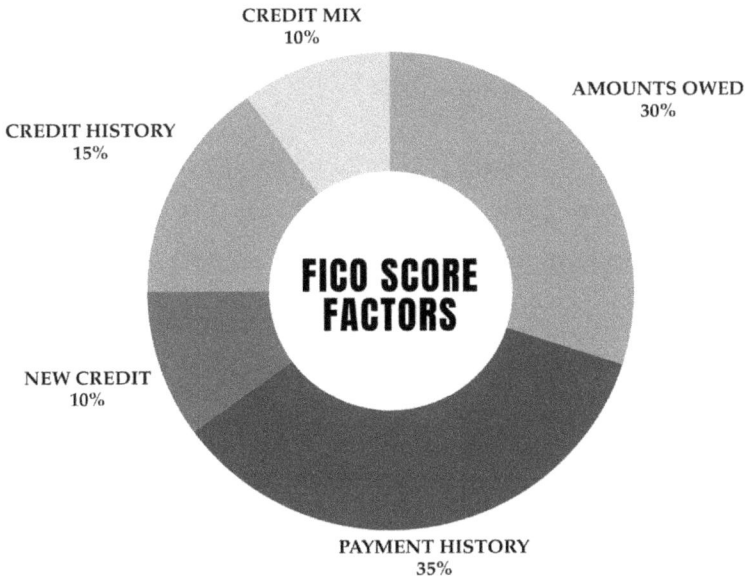

1. Payment History – 35%

This is the single most important factor in your credit score. It reflects how reliably you've paid your past debts. On-time payments help your score go up, while late payments, collections, charge-offs, and bankruptcies can seriously lower it. The more time that passes after a negative event, the less impact it has on your score, especially if you build a strong track record moving forward.

2. Amounts Owed – 30%

Also known as your *credit utilization ratio*, this measures how much of your available credit you're currently using. Lower is better—ideally under **30%**, and under **10%** for optimal scores. For example, if you have a total credit limit of $10,000 and a balance of $2,000, your utilization is 20%. This part of your score applies primarily to revolving accounts (like credit cards), not installment loans (like a car loan or mortgage).

3. Length of Credit History – 15%

This factor looks at how long you've been using credit and how recently your accounts have been active. It includes the age of your oldest account, your newest account, and the average age of all accounts. Longer is better—so keeping older accounts open (especially those in good standing) helps.

4. Credit Mix – 10%

This reflects the variety of credit types you've used responsibly. A healthy mix might include credit cards, student loans, car loans, personal loans, or a mortgage. You don't *need* all of these—but showing you can manage both revolving and installment credit is a plus.

5. New Credit – 10%

This measures how recently you've applied for and opened new credit accounts. Each time you apply for credit, it can trigger a **hard inquiry**, which may lower your score slightly. Several inquiries in a short period, especially for different types of credit, can suggest financial stress or risk. Multiple inquiries for the same loan type– like a mortgage or auto loan–within a short window are usually grouped together and treated as one inquiry.

Final Thought

Your FICO score is dynamic, not permanent—and even small, consistent changes (like paying on time or lowering your utilization) can make a meaningful difference. You don't have to aim for perfection, but understanding the mechanics helps you take control.

Why Your Credit Score Really Matters

Understanding how your credit score is calculated is helpful, but what really matters is how it impacts your everyday life. This three-digit number affects the interest rates you're offered, the loans you qualify for, and how much you'll pay over time. A lower score doesn't just mean a higher rate—it can quietly drain thousands of dollars from your future simply because lenders see you as a higher risk.

EXCEPTIONAL: *800-850*

VERY GOOD: *740-799*

GOOD: *670-739*

FAIR: *580-669*

POOR: *300-579*

Take a car loan, for example. According to 2022 data from Experian, someone with an **800** credit score might qualify for a **6%** interest rate on a used car, while someone with a **600** score could be offered a rate closer to **17%**. On a $25,000 loan paid over six years, that's the difference between a **$415** monthly payment and one around **$556**. Over the life of the loan, the person with good credit would pay less than **$5,000** in interest, while the person with poor credit would pay more than **$15,000**. That's a $141 per month difference—or an extra $10,000—just because of your credit score. This is why I care so much about helping you understand how credit works. It's not about being perfect—it's about making your money go further.

Curious about your credit score? You might already have free access to it through your bank, credit union, or credit card company. Many institutions offer built-in credit score tracking and will even alert you when someone pulls your credit report. For example, I applied for a business credit card recently and received an email about the inquiry within minutes! These alerts can help you catch unauthorized activity early and protect your credit from potential fraud.

If your current accounts don't offer this feature, you can still check your score for free using services like Credit Karma. These platforms typically show a VantageScore, which is slightly different from the FICO score most lenders use. While it's considered "educational," it's still a great way to monitor your progress and spot any big changes over time.

Fixing Your Credit Score

Improving a low credit score takes time, but progress is possible—especially with consistent action. Many people see noticeable changes within **3 to 6 months** if they're paying bills on time, lowering credit card balances, and not taking on new debt they can't manage. More serious issues, like collections or bankruptcies, take longer to recover from. These negative marks can stay on your credit report for up to **7 years**, but their impact fades over time—especially if your recent credit behavior is solid.

Credit Report

Your **credit report** is different from your **credit score**, and it's just as important to understand. While your score is a three-digit number that sums up your creditworthiness, your report is the detailed record behind that number. It includes your accounts, payment history, personal information, and any activity related to your credit over time. I strongly recommend pulling your credit report at least once a year to check it for accuracy. It's one of the easiest ways to catch errors or signs of identity theft before they become bigger problems. Here's what you'll typically find in your credit report:

- Other names you've used (such as maiden names or legal name changes)

- Past addresses and phone numbers

- Former employers

- Details on each account, including balances, credit limits, payment history, and account status

- "Hard" inquiries (credit applications that affect your score)

- "Soft" inquiries (account reviews or pre-approvals that don't affect your score)

- Instructions for disputing inaccurate information

As you review your report, keep an eye out for red flags—like accounts listed as open when they've been closed, late payments you're sure were on time, or unfamiliar accounts you didn't open. If you find an error, it's important to report it to **all three credit bureaus**.

You can access your credit reports for free from **Equifax, Experian, and TransUnion** by visiting www.AnnualCreditReport.com. This is the only federally authorized source for free reports, and you're entitled to one from each bureau every year. Reviewing your reports regularly helps you stay on top of your credit profile, protect against fraud, and simply have a clearer picture of your financial life.

How to Use Different Types of Debt

Credit Cards

At their core, credit cards are tools that allow you to buy something now and pay for it later. If you pay off your balance by the due date, you won't incur interest. However, just because you're not paying interest doesn't mean you're not being impacted in other ways. Numerous studies have shown that people spend significantly more when using credit cards compared to debit cards or cash—anywhere from 12% to 100% more. The reason is that spending on a credit card doesn't feel as tangible.

When we spend cash, we immediately notice less money in our wallet after a purchase. Similarly, when we use a debit card, we see the balance in our bank account decrease within twenty-four hours. However, with credit cards, spending doesn't feel real until it's time to pay the bill. Even if you're able to pay it, you've likely spent more than you would have if the money had been deducted immediately. Another tricky aspect of credit cards is how companies turn them into a game (which they almost always win) by offering points or rewards for spending. Whether it's Amazon, REI, Macy's, or another retailer, we're not truly gaining if we spend 12 to 100% more to get 5% back.

Keep this in mind when using credit cards: Mindfulness around your spending should come first, and savviness about credit card perks should come second.

Car Loans: One Size Doesn't Fit All

Car loans tend to spark strong opinions. Some argue it's a mistake to pay interest on a depreciating asset, while others suggest it's smarter to finance a car and invest your cash instead—potentially earning more than the loan's interest rate. But here's the thing: Both arguments are oversimplified. In the real world, whether financing makes sense depends on your unique situation— your income, credit, savings, and how urgently you need a new vehicle.

Many people use car loans responsibly, taking on manageable payments that fit their budget. And sometimes borrowing isn't about strategy—it's about necessity. If your current car is no longer safe or reliable and repairs don't make financial sense, a loan might be the most practical option.

This was the situation I found myself in as a new mom. When my daughter was a toddler, I was driving a $1,000 Ford Focus—cheap and functional, but not safe. We bought it to avoid debt, but I never felt comfortable driving her in it. After owning the Focus for a short time, we ran the numbers and decided we could afford a loan for a Toyota Camry. Just ten days after buying it, my daughter and I were rear-ended. I had minor whiplash, but my daughter was completely unharmed. I can't say what would've happened in the old car—but I'm grateful we chose safety, even if it meant taking on a loan.

So if you're deciding whether to finance or pay cash, consider the bigger picture:

- Do you have the savings to buy a car outright without draining your emergency fund?

- Is your current car still safe and reliable, or are you buying time on borrowed wheels?

- Would taking on a loan stretch your budget too far, or is it a manageable monthly expense?

If you *need* to borrow, the key isn't whether to finance—it's how much and on what terms. If you *could* pay cash but prefer to finance, ask whether keeping your cash invested or liquid is truly worth the added interest.

If you know a new (or new-to-you) vehicle is in your future, here are two smart ways to prepare:

1. Check your credit score.

The better your score, the better your interest rate—and that can save you thousands over the life of the loan. If your score could use some work, spend a few months improving it before you buy.

2. Start "making payments" now.

Even if your car is paid off, consider setting aside the amount you'd spend on a car payment into a savings account. That way, when you do need to replace your vehicle, you'll have a head start—and maybe even the ability to skip financing altogether.

Student Loans

Student loans are one of the most common forms of debt today—and for many, the only way they can afford college. But once repayment kicks in, student loans can feel less like an opportunity and more like a roommate who never moves out. If you're managing student debt now, you're not alone—and there are ways to make it more manageable.

Start by getting clear on the basics: how much you owe, who your loan servicers are, and whether your loans are federal, private, or both. **Federal loans** offer more flexibility, like income-driven repayment plans and forgiveness programs for those in nonprofit or government work. These can lower your monthly payments, though they may stretch out the timeline and the total interest you'll pay. **Private loans** usually come with fewer perks, but it's still worth asking your lender about hardship options or refinancing—especially if your credit and income have improved. Just be cautious about trading flexibility for a slightly better interest rate.

No matter what kind of loan you have, it helps to run the numbers. For example, a $30,000 loan at 6.5% over 10 years comes to about $340 a month—and nearly $11,000 in interest. Knowing what you're working with makes it easier to build a plan. Even making small extra payments can chip away at that balance and save you money in interest over time. Understanding and proactively managing your student loans takes some work, but it is worth it to put you back in the driver's seat.

Should You Borrow from Your 401(k)?

If you're in a financial pinch, it might be tempting to borrow from your 401(k). After all, it's your money—and the process is often faster and more straightforward than applying for a traditional loan. In some cases, this can be a reasonable short-term solution, especially if you're confident you can repay it quickly and don't have access to better alternatives. The benefits of a 401(k) loan include speed, convenience, and the fact that you're essentially borrowing from yourself. You won't need a credit check, and the interest you pay goes back into your account. It can also be more flexible and cost-effective than high-interest personal loans or credit cards. But it's not without drawbacks.

First, you're taking money out of a tax-advantaged retirement account—money that would otherwise be growing. Say you borrow $10,000 and take a year to repay it. If your investments would've earned 8% during that time, that's $800 in missed growth. Over time, those opportunity costs can add up.

There's also a tax quirk worth noting. If you're borrowing from a Traditional 401(k), you're taking out pretax dollars but repaying the loan with after-tax income. That means you'll be taxed *twice* on the same money: once when you earn it to repay the loan, and again when you withdraw it in retirement.

And perhaps the biggest risk: If you leave your job for any reason, the loan typically becomes due within a short window. If you can't repay it in time, it's treated as an early withdrawal, which means income taxes and potentially a 10% penalty if you're under age 59 1/2.

So is borrowing from your 401(k) ever a good idea? It depends. For a short-term, one-time need—especially if other options are limited—it may be worth considering. But it's important to go in with a plan to repay it quickly and to understand the trade-offs involved. Your future self will thank you.

Borrowing from Family or Friends

Asking your parents for an advance on your allowance as a kid is one thing—asking for a loan as an adult is more complicated. It can feel awkward, emotionally loaded, and risky for the relationship. But with clear expectations and mutual trust, borrowing from family or close friends *can* work in the right situation.

If you're thinking about borrowing money from someone close to you, here are a few things to consider:

- Can they afford to help you without putting themselves at risk? If not, even the best intentions could cause long-term strain—especially if repayment gets delayed.

- What's the current state of your relationship? If things are already rocky, money may create even more tension.

- Could this change the dynamic? For example, if you borrow money for an emergency but then take a vacation before repaying them, how will that be?

- Will this loan help or hurt your financial health overall? Keep in mind that unlike a bank loan, personal loans won't help you build your credit.

If you decide to move forward, treat it like a formal loan—put the agreement in writing and include the amount, repayment timeline, interest (if any), and who's responsible for tracking payments. Clear expectations protect everyone involved.

Medical Debt

Medical debt is its own beast, with rules and protections that often differ from other types of debt. While it can feel overwhelming—especially when it shows up unexpectedly—it may actually be more flexible and manageable than you'd think. If you receive a medical bill, avoid putting it on a credit card unless you're certain you can pay off the full balance by the end of the month. Unlike credit cards, most medical debt doesn't accrue interest right away (though you should always confirm with your provider). Using a high-interest credit card to pay a no-interest bill can end up costing you significantly more over time.

If the amount you owe is more than you are able to pay, call the provider's billing department and ask if you qualify for financial assistance. You might be surprised who qualifies—even middle-income families can receive help. And even if you don't get a discount, most hospitals and clinics offer interest-free payment plans. There's no shame in asking, especially if you dig into your explanation of benefits and spot something like a $30 charge for a single aspirin.

Paying Down Debt

Now that we've walked through how to think about using debt, let's shift to what happens once you already have it: paying it down. Before diving into numbers and strategies, take a moment to ask yourself: *Why does paying off this debt matter to me?* Having a personal reason—one that feels real and motivating—can help you stay focused when the process starts to feel long or discouraging.

Here are a few ways that "why" might sound:
- "I want to be able to say yes to things—like going on a trip or helping someone out—without panicking about my credit card balance."
- "Right now, every paycheck feels like it's already spent. I just want a little breathing room."
- "I'm tired of feeling like I'm treading water. I want to actually make progress, not just stay afloat."

Own Your Situation

Let's be honest—some of the debt you're carrying might not be entirely your fault. Maybe you were never taught about interest rates, or someone made big promises they didn't follow through on. Maybe life threw you curveballs, and you did what you had to do to get through. Even if the debt wasn't your fault, it's still your responsibility now. And while that might feel frustrating or unfair, it's also empowering—because it means you have the ability to change things. I'm proud of you for showing up, doing the work, and choosing to face your finances with honesty and grit.

Killing Your Debt Dead

Now that you've decided what's important about paying off your debt, let's make a plan. Go back to the list of your debts from Chapter 2. Keep making the minimum payments on all of them, but pick one to focus on paying off more aggressively. Choose one of these strategies to decide which one to start with:

- **Debt Snowball:** Pay off your smallest balance first. Once it's gone, take that freed-up payment and apply it to the next-smallest balance. This method gives you early wins, which can boost your motivation. It's a solid approach when your interest rates are fairly similar.

- **Debt Avalanche:** Pay off the debt with the highest interest rate first, regardless of balance. This method saves you the most money over time, especially if you have high-interest debt like credit cards.

Whichever method you choose, stick with it. Debt payoff is a long game—and that's okay. Celebrate your progress. Track your wins. And don't be afraid to recommit to your goals if you hit a rough patch.

When Consolidation Makes Sense

Debt consolidation can be a helpful option if you're juggling multiple payments or paying high interest rates. The idea is to combine several debts into one new loan or credit card—ideally with a lower interest rate and one simple monthly payment. Two common tools for debt consolidation are:

- **Balance transfer credit cards** – These often come with a 0% introductory interest rate for 12 to 21 months, typically offered by major credit card companies. This period is a window to make payments without accruing new interest, applying your payments towards paying off your balance instead of going towards interest. Even if you can't pay off the entire balance during that time, reducing the principal while interest is paused can still save you hundreds—or even thousands—over time. Just be aware of balance transfer fees (usually 3 to 5%) and what the interest rate will be once the promotional period ends.

- **Fixed-rate personal loans** – Available through banks, credit unions, and online lenders, these loans can be used to consolidate multiple debts into one predictable monthly payment, often with a lower rate than high-interest credit cards.

Just know this: Consolidation doesn't erase or reduce your debt—it just repackages it. If the new interest rate is higher than what you're already paying or the loan term stretches your payments out much longer, it may end up costing you more. But if it simplifies your finances or saves you money on interest, it can be a smart move.

Before applying, check your credit score—better scores tend to qualify for better rates—and compare offers from a few sources. You can also use prequalification tools (available on most lender websites) to check potential rates without impacting your credit.

CHAPTER WRAP-UP

Key Takeaways

- Shifting your perspective on debt can be just as important as the financial strategy you use to pay it down.

- Choose a debt payoff strategy that aligns with your financial situation and goals.

- If you get a bill that you cannot pay off in full, reach out to the billing department to ask if they would allow a payment arrangement.

Key Action Items

- Check your credit score.

- Pull your credit report to make sure it's accurate.

- Identify specific actions you can take to improve your credit.

- Choose a debt payoff strategy.

Journal Prompts

- Imagine a life unburdened by debt. How will it feel? What will be different?

- Reflect on your journey with debt up until now. What have you learned?

- Consider the habits or patterns you need to change to achieve financial freedom. What changes do you need to make to have the life you want?

Chapter 8

BUYING A HOUSE

Considerations Around Buying a House

Buying your first home is a common goal in the United States, often viewed as a milestone of success alongside earning a college degree, getting married, and having children. However, just because homeownership is considered the American dream doesn't mean it has to be your dream.

In this chapter, I'll guide you through the key questions to determine if buying a house is the right decision for you–and, if so, how to approach the process. While this chapter won't give you a precise roadmap, it will provide a framework to help you make decisions based on your unique situation and goals.

Finally, I'll walk you through the homebuying process step by step so you'll know what to expect and how to get started.

Question #1: Why Do You Want to Buy a Home?

When it comes to buying a home, it's tempting to jump straight to the "how" and skip over the "why." Don't make that mistake! Understanding your "why" will help you decide whether buying a home is the right choice and will also guide the "how" and "when." Here are five common reasons people want to buy a home:

#1 – Build Wealth

Many people buy a home because they've heard it's a good investment. While real estate can be an excellent wealth-building tool, there's no guarantee it will pay off. It's crucial to understand how homeownership can build wealth and how long the process may take.

Wealth in real estate is ultimately built through equity, which is the difference between a home's market value and the amount owed on it. It grows in two ways: through appreciation (the home's value increasing over time) and by paying down the mortgage. This equity can be leveraged to qualify for loans or "captured" by selling the home and keeping the proceeds.

The following chart shows how the mortgage balance is gradually paid down, while the home value fluctuates but trends upward in the long run. The difference between these two values is the home equity.

GROWING EQUITY

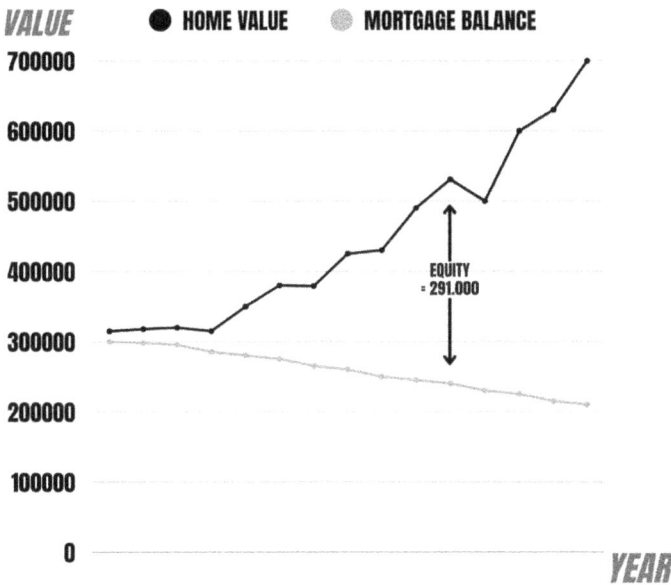

VALUE ● HOME VALUE ◉ MORTGAGE BALANCE

EQUITY = 291,000

YEAR

Homeownership isn't a guaranteed quick path to wealth. In fact, it often takes years before a home can be sold for a profit. This is for two reasons:

1. There are costs associated with both buying and selling a home. These closing costs typically range from 2 to 5% of the home price when buying (*not* including your down payment) and 5 to 10% when selling. For example, if you buy a $400,000 home with 4% closing costs ($16,000) and later sell it with 7% closing costs ($28,000), your home needs to grow in value by $44,000 just to break even.

2. The real estate market doesn't necessarily go up every year. Yes, real estate values have historically risen over time, but this growth isn't guaranteed every year. In fact, in some years, home values have actually

gone down! Selling a home in a down market can result in you actually losing money on your investment or needing to go through foreclosure (where the bank takes back the house) or a short sale (where the bank allows you to sell the house for less than you owe them).

The longer you own your home, the lower the risk of your house value decreasing and the more likely it is to build your wealth.

#2 – Housing Stability

Homeownership can provide a sense of stability, offering the assurance that no one can force you to move out. Mortgage payments are often more consistent than rent, though property taxes and homeowners insurance costs can still cause your mortgage payment to go up.

Staying in one home instead of moving frequently between rentals can also save you money. Each move often comes with expenses such as moving costs and the purchase of new furniture or decor.

#3 – Put Down Roots

Although you can feel a sense of community as a renter, owning your own home often fosters a deeper connection to your neighborhood. Homeownership allows you to invest in your property through upgrades, painting, gardening, and other improvements.

#4 – More Freedom/Control

Homeownership means no more asking a landlord's permission to paint or make changes (though some homes do come with HOA rules). Any improvements you make increase the value of your own property, not someone else's. There's a sense of satisfaction in making a space truly your own.

#5 – Save Money on Your Monthly Payment

Depending on your local housing market and the size of your down payment, you might save money on your monthly payment by buying a home instead of renting. But monthly payments aren't the whole picture—homeownership also comes with maintenance, repairs, insurance, and property taxes. In some cases, owning a home may cost more than renting once those are factored in.

That's why you need to look past the "why rent when you could own?" messaging. With renting, your monthly rent is usually the most you'll pay. With homeownership, your mortgage is just the beginning—unexpected repairs and rising costs can make your actual expenses much higher. Renting offers predictability and flexibility, while owning builds equity and stability. The right choice depends on your goals, finances, and lifestyle.

Question #2: Can You Afford To?

Monthly Payment

The second most important question to ask yourself is whether you can afford the monthly mortgage payment. This payment includes the principal and interest portion of your loan, your property taxes, your homeowners insurance, and, in some cases, private mortgage insurance (PMI).

The principal and interest portion of your mortgage is fixed, but property taxes typically increase annually, as does homeowners insurance. Be sure to allow some wiggle room to account for these rising costs.

Make sure your mortgage doesn't consume so much of your income that you have nothing left to save for retirement or to apply towards other important financial goals. Avoid becoming "house-rich and cash-poor," where all your money is tied up in your home, leaving little to spend or save.

PRO TIP

Most experts recommend spending no more than 30% of your gross income on housing. Some housing markets may necessitate spending more, but that leaves less for everything else.

Down Payment + Upfront Costs

Most mortgage lenders require you to make a down payment ranging from 3% to 20%, depending on the program. Some buyers come up with a down payment by saving their own money, while others are fortunate enough to have a family that is willing and able to gift funds towards the purchase. If you fall into the latter, be sure to track the gifted funds and keep your lender informed.

If you can't afford a down payment out of savings, you may look at using retirement funds, either as a loan or a withdrawal. Keep in mind that borrowing from your 401(k) is not a very tax-efficient option, as you're borrowing pretax funds and repaying them with after-tax funds. You'll need to be sure that you can afford to pay the loan back in addition to making your mortgage payments. If you leave your job, you will likely be required to pay back the loan quickly—and if you can't, it will count as a withdrawal.

If you're under the age of 59 ½, withdrawal of any pretax funds is considered a premature distribution. Not only will the withdrawal be taxed, but it will also be subject to a 10% premature distribution penalty. However, you may qualify for a first-time homebuyer exemption, which waives the 10% penalty on up to $10,000 of withdrawals. Consult a financial advisor or accountant for details.

Aside from the tax ramifications, keep in mind that any money you pull out from your retirement accounts will not be growing for retirement. You may have a hard time catching up to where you were without compound interest working in your favor.

There are circumstances where borrowing or withdrawing from your retirement makes sense for you, just make sure you understand the impacts.

Question #3: Is Now the Right Time?

It was once the societal norm to fall in love, get married, save up, and then buy a home together. Women were not only expected to wait for a man before buying a house but were often required to do so.

Until the Equal Credit Opportunity Act was passed in 1974 (thanks, Ruth Bader Ginsburg!), it was legal to discriminate against women in lending. Women could be denied loans, charged higher interest rates, or need a male co-signer, such as a husband, father, or brother.

Shortly after the act was passed, in 1981, single women homebuyers (11%) surpassed single men homebuyers (10%). Forty years later, in 2023, the National Association of Realtors reported that single women accounted for 19% of homebuyers, while single men made up just 10%. (Can you hear Beyoncé's *Who Run the World*?)

All this to say: Being single does *not* mean you're in a bad life stage to buy a home. If you want to be a homeowner and can afford to, buying a home as a single woman could be a great thing for you!

Maybe you're earning enough to afford it on your own, or maybe you do some "house hacking" and rent out some rooms to help you cover the mortgage, allowing your renters to help grow your equity.

When is it not a good time to buy? One example is during an "in-between" season—when you're unsure about staying in your current job, considering a move to a different area, or facing other major uncertainties in life.

Another life stage that requires extra caution is immediately after a traumatic event, such as a major breakup, the death of a loved one, or another life-altering experience. While buying a home doesn't need to be ruled out entirely, be mindful of committing to a long-term investment if you're not feeling emotionally grounded.

Current Financials (Credit Score, Income, the Market)

While it's important to get clear on why you want to buy a home and whether now is a good time for you to buy, whether or not you'll be able to buy a home depends on your current finances.

For example, a low credit score might prevent you from qualifying for a mortgage. Even if you do qualify, you may not secure the best interest rate, potentially adding hundreds of dollars to your monthly payments.

Your income level is another crucial detail to lenders, as they use your debt-to-income (DTI) ratio to assess how much mortgage you can afford and get approved for.

DEBT TO INCOME RATIO (DTI)

A percentage that displays your financial health to lenders.

MONTHLY DEBT PAYMENTS ÷ **MONTHLY PRETAX INCOME**

50% = *HIGH*

You'll likely be **denied for a loan with a DTI of 50% or higher.*

43% = *LESS FAVORABLE*

36% = TARGET

*You'll likely be **approved** for a loan with a DTI of 35% or lower.*

To calculate your DTI, divide your monthly debt payments (not debt balances) by your monthly pretax income. Pretax income refers to your gross pay before taxes or other deductions are withheld. Keep in mind that different lenders and loan programs have varying criteria. Instead of assuming whether you can qualify for a loan, consult a mortgage lender to explore your options.

Also, be aware that personal loans, like money borrowed from friends or family, typically won't show up in your DTI calculation. But just because they're not counted by a lender doesn't mean they shouldn't count in your own decision making. You're still responsible for repaying that debt, so make sure to include it when assessing how much you can truly afford.

PRO TIP

Don't wait for interest rates to drop.

It's tempting to hold off on buying a home because you're hoping interest rates will go down. But here's the thing—no one can predict where rates are headed, and waiting could mean missing out altogether. Even if rates do drop, so many other buyers are waiting too. That means more competition, more bidding wars, and potentially higher prices. The money you save on interest could get canceled out by what you pay for the home.

If the numbers work for you now and you feel financially solid, don't let the rate keep you on the sidelines. You can always refinance later if rates improve—but if they don't, you'll be glad you didn't wait.

Steps to Buying a House

Now that we've walked through how to decide whether or not to buy a house and if now is the time, let's look at the steps involved in actually buying a house.

Determine Your Budget

Before looking at houses, you'll want to get an idea of what homes you can afford to buy. This depends on how much of a mortgage you can get, what interest rate you're eligible for, and how that monthly payment fits into your overall budget. A mortgage lender can help you with the loan side—but it's up to you to make sure the numbers also work for your real life.

When you meet with a mortgage lender, they'll do a "hard pull" of your credit, which gives them access to your credit score and borrowing history. The good news: Banks expect buyers to shop around, so multiple mortgage-related pulls within a 45-day window only count as one for credit score purposes. These hard pulls can cause a slight dip in your score, but it's worth it to compare rates.

Your lender will also look at your income, debt, and other factors to estimate how much of a loan you will qualify for and how much of a down payment you'll need. But just because a lender says you *qualify* for a loan amount doesn't mean you can *afford* to spend that much. Take time to run your own numbers–look at your monthly income, subtract essentials (like groceries and insurance), and ask yourself what kind of mortgage payment would still leave room for saving, giving, or fun money. That's your real affordability number.

If your credit score or debt-to-income ratio needs work, a good lender can help you strategize—and buying a home might become part of a longer-term plan instead of an immediate step.

Get Preapproved First

If you're ready to start looking at homes, your first step should be getting preapproved by a lender. Preapproval doesn't guarantee final loan approval, but it's a strong signal to sellers (and realtors) that you're a serious buyer. It also gives you a much clearer sense of what's actually in your price range based on your income, credit, debt, and down payment.

Unlike a quick prequalification, which is often based on self-reported info, preapproval involves submitting documentation and going through a credit check. Most realtors won't show homes without a preapproval letter; no one wants to fall in love with a house you can't realistically buy. Here's what lenders typically ask for during the preapproval process:

- Recent pay stubs (usually 30 days' worth)

- Bank statements (2 to 3 months)

- W-2s or tax returns (last 1 to 2 years)

- A copy of your ID

- Permission to pull your credit report

PRO TIP

Don't sabotage your own loan. Once you're preapproved, **hold off on big financial moves** until after closing. That means no new credit cards, no financing furniture, and definitely no major purchases. Even something like buying a new couch on credit can throw off your debt-to-income ratio and jeopardize the whole deal.

Don't sabotage your own loan. Once you're pre-approved, hold off on big financial moves until after closing.

Choose a Great Real Estate Agent

Your agent is going to be in your corner through one of the biggest purchases of your life, so you want someone you genuinely feel comfortable with *and* someone who knows what they're doing. Look for an agent who's familiar with the area you're buying in and has a strong track record of helping clients reach their real estate goals.

Your agent will help narrow your search, set up showings, and evaluate homes with a trained eye. A great agent won't just point out the pretty features—they'll also help you notice potential red flags, like an aging roof, outdated electrical, or a furnace near the end of its life. When it's time to make an offer, they'll guide you in taking smart, calculated risks that balance your desire to be financially wise with the reality of a competitive market. You want someone who can keep you grounded, ask the right questions, and help you make decisions you'll feel good about both now and later.

As tempting as it is to include friends and family in your homebuying journey, make sure you're leaning on your agent. Loved ones often have plenty of advice—but the market has changed a lot since your parents bought their first place. A good agent knows how things work *today* and can help you make smart decisions based on current realities, not outdated tips.

How to Find the Right Agent

Don't be afraid to interview a few agents before choosing one; this is a big decision and the right fit matters. A few good questions to ask:

- How long have you been working in this area?

- What types of clients do you typically work with?

- How do you help buyers navigate competitive markets?

- Can you walk me through what to expect from your process?

- Are you part of a team, or will I be working directly with you?

Last but not least, you'll want to ask how your agent gets paid. Most of the time the seller pays the commission for both their agent and yours—so as a buyer you usually don't pay anything out of pocket. But with some recent rule changes, agents now have to put their payment agreement in writing before they start showing you homes. It's a good idea to ask how your agent gets paid and to be aware if there's any chance you'd owe something– just so there are no surprises later.

The right agent will welcome your questions, explain things clearly, and want you to feel informed every step of the way.

Make an Offer

When you find a home you love, your agent will help you put together a competitive offer. It's not just about the price—sometimes a well-crafted offer gets accepted even if it's not the highest one. Here are some of the factors your agent will walk you through:

- **Purchase price** – How much are you offering the seller for the home?

- **Escalation clause** – This says you're willing to beat another offer by a certain amount up to a set limit. It's a way to stay competitive without overbidding from the start.

- **Earnest money** – A "good faith" deposit you make after your offer is accepted. It stays in escrow until closing. If you walk away for a reason not protected by your contract, the seller may keep it.

- **Closing costs** – These are the costs of finalizing the transaction. They're often paid by the buyer, but in some markets or situations you might be able to negotiate for the seller to cover a portion.

- **Closing date** – You'll usually propose this in your offer, but timing often depends on how quickly your lender can finalize everything. A faster closing can make your offer more appealing—especially if the seller is in a hurry.

- **Contingencies** – These are conditions that protect both sides. Common ones that protect the buyer include a financing contingency (you can back out if your loan falls through) and an inspection contingency (you can walk away if something major turns up during the inspection). Waiving these can strengthen your offer—since there's less risk for the seller—but it adds more risk for you, so it's something to talk through carefully with your agent.

If you're trying to buy in a **seller's market**—meaning there are more buyers than homes available—you may need to take on more risk to make your offer stand out. Your real estate agent will help you understand the risks involved and figure out what you're comfortable with.

One of the most important things to remember is that there's no one "right" way to structure an offer. Buying a home is always a bit of a calculated risk, and the goal is to make informed decisions based on your situation, not someone else's. Once you find the right home and get your offer accepted, your lender will help you submit your loan application and keep everything on track so you can close on time.

Closing Process

Once your offer is accepted, you're officially under contract—but there are still a few important steps to take before you can close and get the keys. First up: **homeowners insurance**. Your lender will require it, but you can choose the insurance agent or company that works best for you. If you're not sure where to start, your real estate agent or lender can usually point you in the right direction.

Next, your **lender will order an appraisal** to make sure the home is worth what you're offering. This step is mostly for the lender's protection and is different from a **home inspection**, which is for *your* peace of mind.

You'll also be working with a **title company** during this part of the process. Their role is to make sure the title is clear (meaning no one else can claim the home), prepare your closing paperwork, and offer **title insurance** just in case any issues come up later. They also manage the **escrow account**, which is where your earnest money and other closing funds are held safely until the day everything is finalized. In some cases you might have more than one title company involved, depending on how the transaction is set up.

As for your move-in date, that's something you and the seller will agree on. Sometimes buyers move in on the day of closing, other times it's before or after—just depends on what works for everyone.

If you're moving in before closing, hold off on big credit purchases—no matter how tempting it is to start furniture shopping. Even something as simple as a new fridge on a payment plan could mess with your loan approval. It's better to wait a little longer than to risk the whole deal falling apart at the finish line.

One way to keep things smooth: Make sure your real estate agent, lender, and title company are all in communication with each other early and often. You're the common thread—so don't assume they're automatically in sync. A quick group email to confirm timelines can save a lot of stress later.

What Can Go Wrong—and What It Means For You

Even when everything seems to be going smoothly, surprises can still pop up. Here are a few common ones to be aware of:

- **The inspection turns up something major** – You might be able to negotiate repairs or walk away, as long as you keep your inspection contingency in place.

- **The home appraises for less than your offer** – You may need to come up with extra cash to cover the gap, since the lender won't loan more than the home is worth.

- **Your financing falls through** – If you didn't include a financing contingency, you could lose your earnest money.

- **The home isn't insurable or has big structural issues** – Your lender might decide not to fund the loan at all, which can derail the purchase.

Example Process of Buying a House

Buying a house is a big step, but breaking it down into manageable stages makes it much easier to navigate. Here's a simplified look at what the process might look like:

EXAMPLE TIMELINE

☑ *Meet with lender for pre-approval*
☑ *Hire agent*
☑ *Shop for homes*
☑ *Make an offer*
☑ *Offer accepted – open escrow*
☑ *Schedule inspection*
☑ *Lender orders appraisal*
☑ *Title company completes title search*
☑ *Finalize loan and sign docs*
☑ *Wire closing funds*
☑ *Close and get keys!*

BUYING A HOUSE

Buying a house is a mix of preparation, teamwork, and calculated risks. Stay informed, work with experts, and focus on what matters most to you. This process may seem daunting, but step by step you'll find the home that's right for you!

CHAPTER WRAP-UP

Key Takeaways

- Get clear on why you want to buy a home before jumping into the process.

- Work with a trusted lender and a knowledgeable real estate agent who can walk you through each step.

- Once you're in the process, avoid making big credit purchases or applying for new credit—it could derail your financing.

Key Actions

- Reach out to a lender to see what steps you need to take to move toward homeownership.

- Interview a few real estate agents and choose someone you feel comfortable with and confident in.

- Make a realistic budget for homeownership that goes beyond the mortgage—include insurance, property taxes, and maintenance so you know the true cost of owning a home.

Journal Prompts

- What messages, positive or negative, do you associate with owning a home versus renting?

- How would owning a home support (or possibly conflict with) your current financial goals and values?

- Imagine your life five years from now. Would you prefer the stability of owning or the flexibility of renting? Why?

"You have to communicate about money to understand each other's values and work towards common financial goals."

—Jean Chatzky

Chapter 9

HOW TO TALK TO YOUR PARTNER ABOUT MONEY

"You may want to google the word *tact*," my friend said when I described an attempt I'd made to bring up a money conversation with my husband. They weren't wrong. I didn't know how to approach the conversation I wanted to have and, well, I bombed it.

I talk a lot about money (like—a lot), but talking about our money with my husband is different. Turns out, money is a loaded topic, even for someone whose entire livelihood revolves around it.

If talking about money with your partner stresses you out, you're not alone! This chapter will provide practical tips to help you and your partner have healthy conversations about money at every stage of your relationship.

Stages

Let's start by looking at some important considerations for each stage of your relationship.

Early Days

One of the first money interactions you'll face is divvying up expenses when you go out. Will you split bills evenly, take turns paying, or come up with another method that works for both of you? These early financial interactions are valuable practice for future money conversations.

As you spend time together, start to notice how your partner talks about and uses money. What do they enjoy spending on? When they discuss money, do they mention saving or investing? Generally speaking, do they make plans for their future and take actionable steps towards their goals?

As your relationship progresses, you will gradually share more personal financial details with each other. At some point, you will likely share what debt you have, if you have savings or investments, your credit situation, etc. There's not necessarily a "right" time for this conversation, but it's best to have it before combining finances.

Getting Serious

The more serious your relationship gets, the more your personal finances will increasingly affect each other. You may progress from splitting a restaurant bill and plane tickets to sharing rent and groceries. You'll make decisions about where to live and what financial commitments to take on based on your shared financial situation.

Eventually, you'll want to have a conversation about whether to combine your finances and how to do so.

You and your partner bring different lived experiences to the relationship, such as how you observed your parents manage money with their partner and whether you've combined finances with a partner in the past. Fortunately, there are many ways to manage your money together, and you have the freedom to choose what works best for you!

Buckets

Early in your relationship, you'll likely use the two-bucket system, where each of you maintain your own bank accounts and don't have any shared accounts. This system is common in the early stages of a relationship, and couples may continue using this system if they don't fully trust their partner or if they have experienced financial or other trauma in a past relationship. While this separation may feel safer, it requires more effort to divide expenses and deciding who pays what bills.

TWO BUCKET SYSTEM

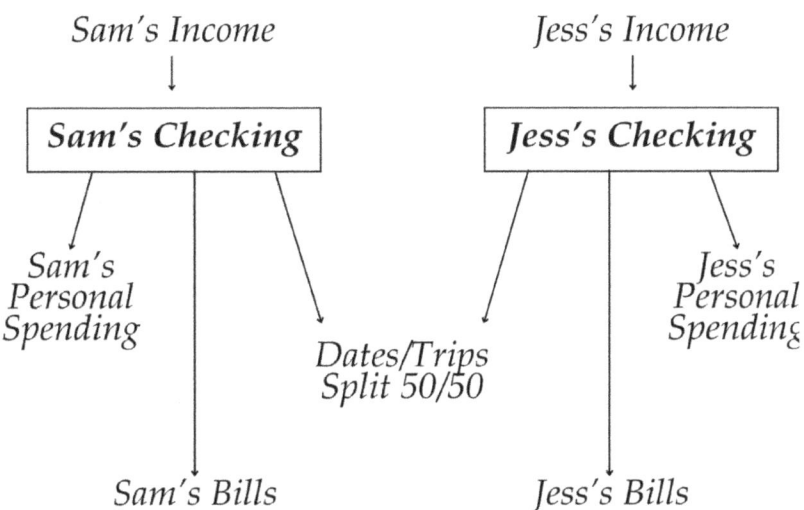

Another common system is the one-bucket system, where you combine all your money in jointly owned accounts, with all your income going into the shared account(s). All income is deposited into the shared account(s) and all expenses are paid from these accounts.

The one-bucket system is more common among married couples, especially for younger couples and first marriages. This system requires a high level of trust in your partner and does not allow for as much financial autonomy. Both partners have full access to all shared money, along with complete transparency around spending.

ONE BUCKET SYSTEM

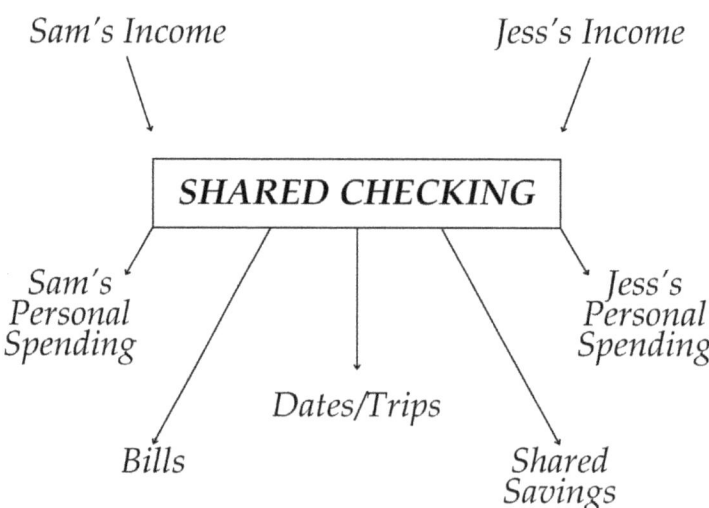

Lastly is the three-bucket system, which incorporates shared accounts in addition to individual accounts. You might deposit all income into the shared account, then transfer an agreed-upon amount into your individual accounts for personal spending. Alternatively, you may deposit all income into individual accounts and transfer a set amount—either a fixed sum or a percentage of your income—into the shared account.

THREE BUCKET SYSTEM

Version 1

Sam's Income

Jess's Income

Sam's Checking

Jess's Checking

Sam's Personal Spending

60% of Sam's Income

60% of Jess's Income

Jess's Personal Spending

Sam's Bills

Jess's Bills

SHARED CHECKING

Dates/ Trips

Shared Bills

Shared Savings

THREE BUCKET SYSTEM

Version 2

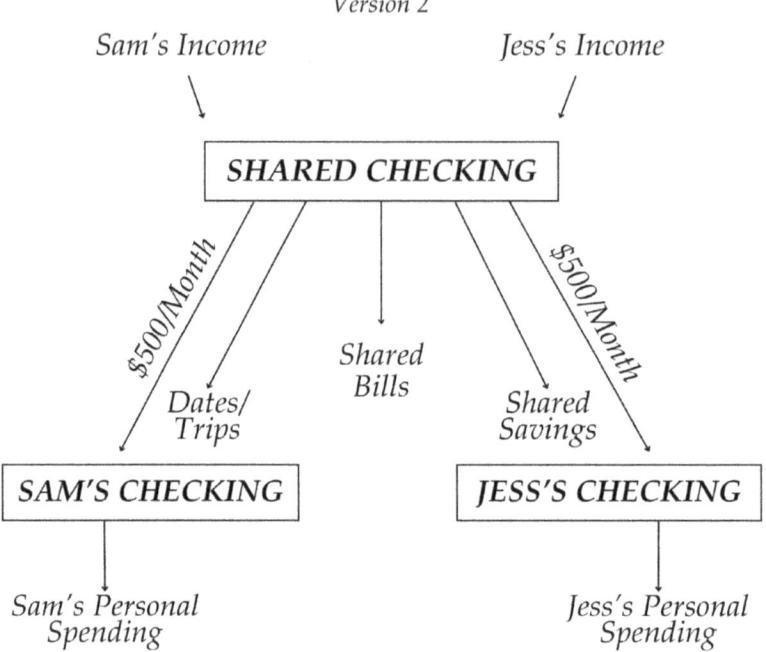

Private Money vs. Secret Money

Regardless of what system you use, it's important to understand the difference between private money and secret money.

Private money refers to money that your partner is aware of but doesn't have access to or visibility of. This could include funds in your individual checking account or cash withdrawal from a joint account.

Secret money, on the other hand, is not agreed upon and is intentionally kept hidden from the other partner. It can include hidden income, spending, accounts, or debt—which the other partner may be responsible for even if they're unaware of it!

Understanding this distinction matters because secret money can erode trust and lead to deeper conflict, while private money can support autonomy within an honest relationship.

Guardrails

Next, let's talk about one tool that can make those conversations a whole lot easier: guardrails. Guardrails are financial boundaries–defined expectations of what's okay and what isn't. Establishing shared financial guardrails is a great way to uncover and address the "unspoken rules" you both bring into the relationship.

Unspoken rules are implicit expectations and norms that are assumed but not explicitly communicated—you might not even realize you have them! These unspoken rules are formed in large part by how things were for you growing up.

Perhaps it was normal in your household to carry credit card balances–not desirable, but normal. Maybe you grew up hearing, "Always pay yourself first," and now have a default expectation to save no matter how tight your finances are. Or maybe saving for retirement was something reserved for "those people" who make a lot of money and can afford to invest.

Regardless of what unspoken rules you bring into the relationship, discussing them openly and creating shared guardrails can help prevent misunderstandings and maybe even avoid some conflicts.

Here are a few examples of financial guardrails you may set together:

- Check with each other before spending over a certain amount.

- Aim to donate a fixed percentage of income to charity.

- Avoid applying for credit without discussing it first.

- If someone asks for money, take 24 hours before answering.

These guardrails may change over time. For example, your "check before spending" amount might start at $100 then increase as your income grows. Or perhaps you need new guardrails to deal with changing family dynamics. As you and your circumstances change, continue revisiting and discussing your guardrails.

PRO TIP

In every stage, in every money conversation, practice curiosity over criticism. Resist the urge to jump to blame or shame or to try to prove why you're right. If you see emotions as clues, curiosity can turn money conversations into an opportunity to get to know each other better.

Who Does What

Once you've set some financial guardrails, the next step is figuring out who's handling what. There are five main areas of financial responsibility to cover, and how you divide them is totally up to you. You might choose roles based on who has more time, who enjoys certain tasks, or simply who's better at them. You can also rotate responsibilities from time to time to make sure you both stay in the loop.

1. **Planning and Tracking Spending:** This responsibility involves forecasting how much money will flow in and out of each category and comparing actual income and expenses to the plan.

2. **Bill Paying:** Decide who will be responsible for paying the bills and setting up a system to ensure they are paid on time. Both partners should understand the system, even if only one person handles its implementation.

3. **Saving and Investing:** You'll want to discuss and set your saving and investing goals together and designate one partner to handle tasks like setting up automatic contributions or shopping for better interest rates.

4. **Insurance:** Work together to decide what insurance you need and how much coverage to get. One of you can take the lead on researching options or communicating with insurance agents.

5. **Debt:** It's essential for both partners to understand how much debt you have and what your interest rates are. One person can manage tasks like setting up automatic payments, negotiating with creditors, and exploring alternative options such as loan consolidation.

Navigating Financial Differences

It's common for couples to have different financial styles—one person may be naturally inclined to save while the other leans toward spending or living in the moment. These differences don't have to be deal breakers, but they do require compassion, curiosity, and compromise.

Try to understand *why* your partner thinks the way they do about money. Are they motivated by security? Freedom? Scarcity? Past experiences? Getting curious (rather than critical) about the "why" helps you work *with* each other instead of against each other. Financial therapists often recommend practices like:

- Naming your shared values first (for example, freedom, security, generosity)

- Using those values to shape your goals together

- Setting a "fun money" amount so each partner has autonomy even if one is the saver and the other the spender

Remember: Compromise doesn't mean splitting the difference—it means building something that truly works for both of you.

What If One of You Doesn't Work for Pay?

Stay-at-home parents and nonearning partners still contribute immensely to the household. Whether through caregiving, emotional labor, or managing daily logistics, that contribution deserves financial recognition and respect. Here are a few ways to reflect that in your planning:

- Ensure access to shared bank accounts

- If you're married, consider contributing to a retirement account for the non-earning spouse (such as a spousal IRA), using the income of the earning partner to qualify.

- A healthy financial partnership means both voices carry equal weight, regardless of who earns what.

Money Conflict Cycle

Do you find that you and your partner tend to have the same money fights over and over—like a record stuck on repeat? One of you may be triggered by something small and seemingly irrelevant, sparking an argument. In response, one or both of you may react in harmful ways, with one partner eventually shutting down or walking away in despair. When these patterns persist, it can feel hopeless and make you question whether having the conversation is even worth it.

The key to breaking the cycle is identifying its distinct stages and understanding how they play out so you can proactively disrupt the pattern.

Here are the stages:

- **Trigger or Initial Disagreement:** The cycle begins with a trigger, such as one partner overspending, which sets the process in motion.

- **Emotional Response:** The other partner reacts emotionally, perhaps feeling angry, anxious, or frustrated.

- **Thoughts:** The reacting partner assigns meaning to their partner's actions, making assumptions or generalizations like, "They always do this," or "They must not care about our financial goals."

- **Behavior:** The reacting partner responds to the trigger based on their thoughts and emotions, perhaps criticizing their partner or walking out. This behavior can then trigger the other partner, perpetuating the cycle.

To break this money conflict cycle once you've recognized the pattern, you can start by owning your own role in the dynamic. Note what triggers you and how you respond. When you're able, create a safe space for your partner to share their perspective and practice curiosity over criticism as they speak.

You may find it helpful to share your money stories with each other to better understand what past experiences are shaping your financial perspectives. If you find you're unable to have a healthy dialogue with each other, you may find it helpful to work with a therapist to address your money conflict cycles.

Life Goals

If you haven't already, you and your partner may find it helpful to discuss your shared long-term goals. Are you on the same page regarding major life events like buying a house, having children, and where you want to live? Don't make assumptions on important issues like these—not everyone wants to be a homeowner, a parent, or live in the same location indefinitely.

Emergency Funds and Insurance

As you intertwine your lives financially—such as by sharing a lease or loan—consider building a shared emergency fund and obtaining life insurance to protect each other. Even if you aren't legally bound by marriage, you rely on each other financially, and what happens to one of you affects both of you.

Putting a Ring on It

Planning on getting married? Congratulations, this is an exciting time! You likely already have a Pinterest board created and perhaps you've started shopping venues. If you don't have a shared bank account yet, this is a great time to set one up. You can use it for wedding expenses and later incorporate it into whichever system you choose to adopt.

This is a great time to start working with a third person on your plans to merge finances. You may find it beneficial to connect with a couples therapist, a spiritual leader, or a financial advisor. Getting insight from a professional early in this transition can help set you up for success by anticipating challenges and setting shared expectations.

Legal Implications

Getting married is rarely discussed in legal terms, but the reality is that marriage may be the most significant legal contract you'll ever enter. By tying the knot, you and your partner essentially become business partners. Moving forward, your spouse's finances, including debts, will become intertwined with yours to some extent.

Your state of residence determines how your property is treated when you are married. If you live in a community-property state, all the assets and debts accrued during your marriage are considered shared. It doesn't matter who earned the money, made the financial decisions, or took on the debt. If you'd like to make your own arrangements as to how your assets and debt will be treated in your marriage, you can legally document them in a prenuptial agreement. It's highly advisable to consult a legal professional about a prenup, especially if you're entering the relationship with disproportionate assets.

One exception to community property is inheritance. If an inheritance is kept separate and never commingled—such as by adding a spouse to the title or depositing it into a shared bank account—it is typically considered separate property.

If you live in a separate-property state, assets and liabilities acquired in your name are considered separate property, regardless of whether they were acquired before, during, or after the marriage. While this protects you from liabilities your spouse incurs, it also means you won't have access to any accounts that are only in your spouse's name. If you want assets to be shared, ensure they are titled accordingly.

PRO TIP

The treatment of your assets and liabilities is determined on your state of residence, not the state where you were married. Keep this in mind if you move or expect to move down the road.

One last note: This may be surprising, but there are circumstances in which marital law applies to you even if you've never been officially married. Some states recognize common-law marriage, which may apply to your relationship if you do "married people things" such as living together or raising children together.

Money Dates

A great way to stay on the same page is to schedule money dates with your partner–ideally at least once a month. Once you get into a routine, these dates shouldn't take longer than an hour and should be planned at a mutually agreeable time. Except for urgent matters, it's helpful to save all your money-related conversations for this time, especially if one of you struggles to engage in money conversations.

Be mindful of your environment—remove distractions such as phones, screens, or other people to the best of your ability. You might enhance the atmosphere by pouring a favorite drink, lighting a candle, or playing relaxing music.

Agenda

To make the most of your time together, prepare an agenda and make it accessible to both of you. You could have a list on the fridge or a shared note on your phones. Here are the key items to include on your agenda:

- Review account balances:
  - Do any transfers need to be made?
  - Are we on track to meet our saving and investing goals?
- Review spending:
  - What spending patterns do you notice?
  - Are there any transactions that look unusual or subscriptions that need to be canceled?
  - How could more money be allocated to value categories?
- Look ahead:
  - What upcoming events or expenses need discussion? Think holidays, birthdays, travel, large purchases, etc.

- Action items:

    o Who is responsible for what, and by when?

The goal of these meetings is to have dedicated time to ensure these conversations happen and to break down big goals into manageable bite-sized action items. The more consistently these dates happen, the easier they'll become! Before you know it, money will be a source of unity in your relationship.

Look for a Partner, Not a Prince

In the quest for financial stability, it's important to find a partner, not a prince. A "prince" may be charming and promise to provide and take care of you, but relying on a man as a financial plan can have negative consequences, such as reduced earnings and loss of financial autonomy. A partner, by contrast, supports mutual growth and shared responsibilities. By working together, you can ensure that your goals and dreams are respected and pursued as a team.

Staying involved in your finances is crucial to maintaining security and independence. Understanding where your money is going, how it's growing, and what risks it faces allows you to make informed decisions with your partner. Financial literacy also prepares you for life's unexpected challenges and builds confidence in managing your money. Ultimately, it's not about the dollars and cents—it's about fostering confidence and the freedom to live the life you want.

PRO TIP

A man is not a financial plan (and neither is a woman, for that matter).

Financial Abuse

I want to briefly touch on the topic of financial abuse so you can recognize and protect yourself from it. While not often talked about, it is surprisingly common. One *U.S. News & World Report* survey found that nearly 22% of respondents had experienced financial abuse in a past relationship, and 14% said they were currently in a financially abusive situation. It coincides with nearly all domestic violence instances and is a common reason that women stay in abusive relationships.

> **A man is not a financial plan. (Neither is a woman, for that matter).**

What Is Financial Abuse?

Financial abuse occurs when money is used as a tool of control, manipulation, or exploitation within a relationship. It often coexists with other forms of abuse, but it can also happen on its own. Cultural norms, such as the belief that one partner should exclusively handle finances, can sometimes enable these dynamics.

Examples of financial abuse:

- Excluding you from financial decisions or making them without your consent.
- Limiting access to money by withholding cash, cards, or login details for bank accounts.
- Taking out debt in your name without your knowledge or permission.
- Intentionally damaging your credit score.
- Preventing you from getting a job or earning income.
- Refinancing loans or retitling assets without your agreement.
- Diminishing your financial independence so that you are dependent on them.

What Should You Do?

Protect Yourself: Stay engaged with your finances. Know where your money is, where it's going, and remain involved in financial decisions to reduce vulnerability to financial abuse.

Seek Help: If you suspect financial abuse, organizations like the National Domestic Violence Hotline can provide resources and support. Search for "financial abuse" on their website for specific guidance.

If you're experiencing financial abuse, you are not alone. Help is available, and taking even small steps toward financial independence can empower you to regain control over your life. You deserve safety, respect, and financial freedom.

CHAPTER WRAP-UP

Key Takeaways

- Lead with curiosity not criticism.

- Private money isn't the same as secret money—transparency matters.

- Financial abuse is more common than we think. Know the signs and ask for help if you need it.

Key Action Items

- Put your money dates on the calendar to make them part of your routine.

- Choose the bucket system that fits your relationship best.

- Work together to create financial guardrails that feel fair and clear.

- Decide who will take the lead on each area of your shared finances.

Journal Prompts

- What unspoken money rules might you be bringing into your relationship from childhood?

- How has money impacted your current or past relationships? What would you like to do differently moving forward?

- How do you and your partner currently make financial decisions, and how would you like that process to look in the future?

"Insurance is the embodiment of preparedness, offering a safety net when life takes an unexpected turn."

—Unknown

Chapter 10

INSURANCE

Let's face it—insurance isn't the most exciting topic. It's one of those adulting tasks we all know we "should" do, but it often gets pushed to the back burner. But here's the thing: Insurance is really just a way to protect what matters most—your health, your home, your income, your loved ones. It gives you the ability to weather hard things without being financially devastated. You don't buy insurance because you expect the worst; you buy it so the worst-case scenario doesn't ruin you.

In this chapter, we'll break down key types of insurance you might need, why they matter, and how to decide what kind (and how much) to get.

Health Insurance

Health insurance helps protect you from the high costs of medical care by sharing expenses for things like doctor visits, prescriptions, surgeries, and more. You (and possibly your employer) pay a monthly premium to an insurance provider, and when you need care the insurance company helps cover some or all of the cost.

Most plans include a few key features:

Deductible – This is what you pay out of pocket before your insurance starts helping. For example, if your deductible is $1,000, you'll pay the first $1,000 in medical bills yourself. Some services, like annual wellness visits, may still be covered before you hit that number.

Copayments – These are small, flat fees you pay for certain services, like $40 for a doctor visit or $20 for a prescription.

Coinsurance – Once you've met your deductible, coinsurance kicks in. This means you pay a percentage of the cost and your insurance pays the rest. For example, with 30% coinsurance, you'd pay 30% of a bill and insurance covers the other 70%.

Out-of-pocket maximum – This is the most you'll have to pay in a year for covered care. Once you hit that limit, insurance pays 100% of eligible costs for the rest of the year. It's your financial safety net in case of big medical bills.

In-network vs. out-of-network – Most plans have a network of preferred providers. You'll save money by staying in-network. Going out-of-network often means higher costs—or your insurance might not cover it at all.

How It All Comes Together

Let's say you break your ankle. You go to an in-network clinic and pay a $40 copay to see the doctor. They send you for an X-ray that costs $400. If you haven't met your deductible yet, you'll pay the full $400 yourself. You end up needing surgery that costs $10,000. You pay the rest of your $1,000 deductible, then your insurance starts sharing the cost. With 20% coinsurance, you pay 20% of the remaining $9,000—that's $1,800—and insurance covers the rest. If everything you've paid adds up to your plan's out-of-pocket max, anything else you need that year—like follow-ups or physical therapy—would be fully covered by insurance.

Knowing how these pieces work together can help you plan ahead and avoid surprise bills. If you have a nonurgent procedure coming up—like getting a mole removed, doing physical therapy, or even switching medications—it's worth checking where you stand with your deductible and out-of-pocket max. Once you meet your deductible for the year, it might make sense to schedule care before your plan resets. Understanding the timing and structure of your health plan gives you more control—and helps you make financial decisions with fewer surprises.

Health Savings Accounts (HSAs)

A Health Savings Account (HSA) is a tax-advantaged account designed to help you pay for medical expenses. It's only available if you're enrolled in a **high-deductible health plan (HDHP)**, a type of insurance that has lower monthly premiums but higher out-of-pocket costs. You can open an HSA through your employer or on your own, as long as you're eligible. These accounts are especially helpful if you have relatively low healthcare needs or if your employer contributes on your behalf. HSAs come with triple tax benefits:

- **Tax-deductible contributions** – Lowers your taxable income.

- **Tax-free growth** – You can invest your balance and let it grow tax-free.

- **Tax-free withdrawals** – As long as you use the money for qualified medical expenses, it's never taxed.

HSA funds roll over year to year, and the account is yours to keep even if you change jobs or retire. It can also be used as a powerful long-term savings tool for future medical expenses, including in retirement. A helpful goal is to keep at least enough in your HSA to cover your annual deductible.

Flexible Spending Accounts (FSAs)

A Flexible Spending Account (FSA) is another type of pretax account for medical expenses, but it works differently than an HSA. FSAs are only available through an employer, and the funds typically don't roll over long-term. FSAs can be a great fit for predictable, short-term expenses like prescriptions, glasses, or dental work. Just keep in mind:

- You can't invest FSA funds.

- You must use the money within the plan year or risk losing it (some employers offer a short grace period or allow a small amount to carry over).

- You don't need to have a high-deductible plan to qualify.

Health Reimbursement Arrangements (HRAs)

A Health Reimbursement Arrangement (HRA) is an employer-funded account that helps cover out-of-pocket healthcare costs. You can't contribute to an HRA yourself—only your employer can fund it—and they decide how much to put in and what expenses are eligible. HRAs are not portable, which means if you leave your job, the unused money usually doesn't go with you. But while you're employed, it can be a great way to reduce your out-of-pocket medical expenses.

Quick recap:

- **HSA** – Available with HDHPs; owned by you; can invest and save long-term.

- **FSA** – Employer-only; use-it-or-lose-it; good for predictable yearly costs.

- **HRA** – Employer-funded; not portable; helps offset healthcare expenses while you're working.

Choosing the Right Health Plan

One of the most important things to check when reviewing health insurance options is whether your healthcare providers are **in-network**. This includes your primary care doctor, therapist, chiropractor, or anyone else you see regularly. Using out-of-network providers can lead to much higher out-of-pocket costs—or no coverage at all. Don't assume that someone who was in-network last year still is. Providers can change what insurance they accept, and plans can shift their networks too. It's worth double-checking each year—especially if you have a major procedure or ongoing care coming up. You'll also want to pay attention to the type of plan you're choosing. Two of the most common are:

- **HMO (Health Maintenance Organization)** – Lower premiums, but you're usually required to stay in-network and you may need a referral to see a specialist. Great if you want to keep costs down and don't mind a more structured approach.

- **PPO (Preferred Provider Organization)** – Higher premiums, but more flexibility. You can usually see specialists directly and go out-of-network if needed (though it'll cost more).

Whichever plan you choose, don't just look at the monthly premium. Consider your **total annual cost**, including: premiums (what you pay every month), deductible, copays and coinsurance, and out-of-pocket maximum. If you're leaning toward a low-cost, high-deductible plan, make sure you also budget for higher medical costs throughout the year—and fully fund your HSA or emergency savings to cover any surprises.

Auto Insurance

Auto insurance is a form of protection that helps cover the costs if you're in an accident or something happens to your car—like theft, vandalism, or storm damage. You pay a monthly premium, and if you're in an accident or your car is damaged, your insurance can help cover the costs—depending on the type of coverage you have. Keep in mind that you'll need to pay your deductible before insurance starts covering the rest.

Unlike health insurance, auto insurance **doesn't** cover routine maintenance or major mechanical repairs—things like oil changes, new brakes, or engine problems are on you. Here are the types of auto insurance:

- **Liability Coverage** – Covers damage or injuries you cause to others or their property. This is usually required by law.

- **Collision Coverage** – Pays for damage to your own car after an accident, regardless of who's at fault.

- **Comprehensive Coverage** – Covers noncollision incidents like theft, vandalism, or natural disasters.

- **Uninsured/Underinsured Motorist Coverage** – Protects you if you're hit by someone with little or no insurance.

Choosing the Right Coverage

Think about what you need coverage *for*. If you're a safe driver with an older vehicle, you might choose to carry liability-only coverage, which covers damage you cause to others but not your own car. It's more affordable, but it also means you're on your own if your car is damaged or totaled. Even if your car isn't worth much, if you don't have collision or comprehensive coverage and it's totaled in an accident or stolen, you'll need to come up with the cost of a replacement on your own. Kind of like choosing a low-cost health plan—if you go light on insurance, it's even more important to beef up your emergency savings.

If you have a newer vehicle or just want more peace of mind, you'll probably want both collision and comprehensive coverage. Shop around for quotes, and don't forget to ask about discounts—many insurers offer lower rates if you're a good student, bundle with renters or homeowners insurance, or have a clean driving record.

Renters Insurance

What would it actually cost to replace everything you own if your place was broken into or damaged in a fire? Most people don't think about it until something happens. That's where renters insurance comes in. It's a simple, affordable way to protect your stuff *and* cover other unexpected costs. Most policies include three key types of coverage:

- **Personal Property Coverage** – Helps pay to replace your belongings if they're lost, stolen, or destroyed by a covered event like a fire, theft, or natural disaster.

- **Liability Coverage** – Pays for legal or medical expenses if someone is injured in your home or if you accidentally cause damage to someone else's property.

- **Additional Living Expenses (ALE)** – Covers temporary housing, meals, and other costs if your home becomes unlivable due to a covered loss.

Why Renters Insurance Matters

Despite all these benefits, only about **55% of renters** carry renters insurance, according to a recent industry report. That's surprising, especially considering the average policy costs just around $15 to$25 per month. You might think you don't own much of value—but if you had to replace everything at once, the cost would add up fast. Think about what it would take to replace your wardrobe, electronics, and kitchen gear all at once. Even just your shoes at full price might surprise you!

A Real-Life Example

A friend of mine owns a rental property that was damaged in a fire a few years ago. While their landlord insurance covered the building, the tenants didn't have renters insurance. That meant they lost nearly all of their belongings and had no coverage for temporary housing. They didn't have to pay rent during repairs, but they also didn't have a place to stay or funds to replace what they'd lost. If they'd had renters insurance, it would've covered both.

How to Get Renters Insurance

Renters insurance is simple and affordable. You can often add it to your auto insurance policy or buy it separately from the same provider. To figure out how much coverage you need, do a basic inventory and estimate the cost to replace your:

- Furniture
- Clothing
- Electronics
- Kitchen equipment and small appliances
- Bedding and towels
- Sports or hobby gear (bikes, musical instruments, etc.)

Document What You Own

If you ever have to file a claim, remembering—and proving—what you owned can be tough. That's why it's a good idea to create a simple home inventory. You can use a worksheet, take photos or videos, or try a home inventory app.

This practice is also helpful for homeowners, since homeowners insurance covers similar risks.

Life Insurance

Life insurance might feel like a strange expense—you're paying for something you hope you'll never use. However, it's an essential safety net to ease the financial burden on your loved ones if you pass away. There are two primary types of life insurance: term and permanent.

Term Life Insurance

Term life insurance is the simplest and most affordable type of life insurance. With a term policy, you receive a specific amount of coverage for a set number of years (the term) at a fixed rate (your premium). The insurance company cannot change your rate or coverage during this term. However, once the term ends, renewing the policy may not be guaranteed, and if renewal is offered, it will come at a higher rate. Term life insurance does not build cash value—it is insurance only.

Permanent Life Insurance

Permanent life insurance provides coverage indefinitely and comes in two forms: whole life and universal life.

- **Whole Life Insurance:** This type of policy offers a fixed death benefit (the amount paid to your family when you pass) and consistent monthly premiums, making it easy to plan for.

- **Universal Life Insurance:** This option is more flexible. You can adjust both your premiums and the death benefit over time, making it adaptable to your changing needs.

To summarize, term insurance is the cheapest way to get life insurance for a fixed period of time and does not build cash value. Permanent insurance (both whole and universal) will be more expensive, but also builds cash value and does not expire, so long as you keep up with the payments.

When Should You Get Life Insurance?

The best time to get life insurance is before you think you need it. Here are three reasons to consider getting life insurance while you're young and healthy (and feel like you don't need it):

1. It's more affordable when you're young and healthy.

2. Even young people can die unexpectedly.

3. As your life evolves—having kids, buying a house, or starting a business—your need for life insurance will increase but may not be top of mind.

Carrie's Story

Carrie and her husband Brandon had two young children. They purchased life insurance for Brandon, the primary earner, but not for Carrie, since her income wasn't relied upon. They didn't see a need to pay more in life insurance.

Tragically, Carrie was hit by a drunk driver, and after spending two weeks on life support, died at the young age of 35. Brandon needed to take time off work to be with Carrie and care for their children. The family ended up with a trifecta of medical bills, reduced income, and additional expenses, including funeral costs. A family friend started a GoFundMe campaign to help, but it wasn't enough to ease the immediate burden or ongoing financial need. This situation highlights the importance of planning for the unexpected, even when it feels unthinkable.

The best time to purchase a policy is when you're young and healthy.

Takeaway: Get life insurance before you think you need it. Even if no one depends on you financially now, that could change in the future. The best time to purchase a policy is when you're young and healthy.

Don't Rely Solely on Employer-Provided Coverage

Many people assume that the life insurance provided through their employer is sufficient. While employer-offered coverage can be a convenient option, it's not always enough. Here are key considerations:

- The coverage offered may not meet your financial needs.
- You could lose coverage if you change jobs or if your employer discontinues offering life insurance.
- It may not actually be cheaper than obtaining your own policy.

Advice: Treat employer-provided life insurance as supplemental coverage. Get a personal policy that fully meets your needs for long-term financial security.

How much Life Insurance do I need?

The right amount of life insurance depends on your situation and who depends on you financially. At a minimum, you'll want enough to cover basics like funeral costs and a few months of rent so your roommates or loved ones aren't left scrambling. A mid-range option is to buy coverage that would allow your family three to five years of breathing room, giving them time to grieve and adjust without immediate financial pressure. At the higher end, some people choose enough insurance to fully replace their income so their family can maintain the same standard of living without making any financial adjustments. The best approach is to think about what level of support would give your loved ones the most peace of mind.

Disability Insurance

Disability insurance helps protect your income if you're unable to work due to illness or injury, typically covering up to 60% of what you normally earn. While it's often overlooked, disability needs are much more common than you might think. About 1 in 4 Americans will experience a disability before retirement age—some for a short time, some for much longer. That's why this kind of coverage matters.

Two Main Types: Short-Term and Long-Term

Short-Term Disability

Short-term disability usually kicks in for conditions lasting a few weeks to several months. Think recovery from surgery, complications from childbirth, or a broken bone that keeps you off your feet. Another way to cover this kind of short-term disruption is a solid emergency fund with 3 to 6 months of expenses.

Long-Term Disability

Long-term disability covers the bigger, more lasting stuff—like cancer, major injuries, severe arthritis, or mental health conditions that take you out of the workforce for an extended period. A few terms to know when you're looking at disability insurance coverage:

- **Elimination Period:** This is how long you wait after becoming disabled before the benefit starts paying out, often somewhere between 90 to 180 days. A longer elimination period means you'll be covering your own financial needs for longer but also lowers your monthly premium.

- **Benefit Period:** This is how long you'll receive income if you can't work. You can pick something like 5 or 10 years, or coverage all the way to retirement age, like 60 or 65. The longer the benefit, the higher the cost.

- **Note:** Long-term disability insurance is not the same as long-term care insurance. Disability coverage replaces lost income. Long-term care helps pay for help with daily living (like dressing or bathing) if you're unable to care for yourself, usually later in life.

What About Social Security Disability?

You've probably heard of people "on disability" through Social Security. That system does exist—but it's hard to qualify for and the benefits aren't great.

- Most applications take close to a year to process.

- Over 60% are denied on the first try.

- The average monthly benefit is just $950 to $1,100—not enough to live on for most people.

- There's no federal short-term disability benefit, though some states offer limited programs.

Bottom line: it's a backup, not a plan.

What If My Employer Offers Disability Insurance?

Employer-provided disability insurance can be a solid perk, just make sure you're aware of the details:

- If your employer pays the premium, or you pay with pretax funds from your paycheck, any disability benefits you receive will be taxable.

- Group plans are priced based on the overall risk of everyone enrolled—so if you're younger or healthier you might find a better deal on your own.

CHAPTER WRAP-UP

Key Takeaways

- Insurance isn't about expecting the worst—it's about making sure the worst doesn't derail your life.

- Don't rely on GoFundMe or good luck to carry you through a crisis.

- Life insurance is most affordable when you're young and healthy.

- Employer coverage (health, disability, life) is helpful, but it often isn't enough on its own.

Key Actions

- Review your health insurance plan, including your deductible, out-of-pocket max, and whether your providers are in-network.

- Check with your auto insurance agent that your coverage fits your needs.

- If you rent and don't already have renters insurance, get a policy.

- If you're a homeowner, review your homeowners insurance policy and consider updating your home inventory.

- Start a digital inventory of your belongings.

- Get your own life insurance policy if you don't already have one.

Journal Prompts

- What comes up for you emotionally when you think about getting life insurance? Are there beliefs, fears, or assumptions behind that feeling?

"Only put off until tomorrow what you are willing to die having left undone."

—Pablo Picasso

Chapter 11

DO I REALLY NEED A WILL?

"Do you have a will yet?" I once asked a friend. (Yes, I really ask questions like this in real life.)

"No," he said. "I looked up who would get my retirement accounts and custody of the kids if my wife and I died. It already goes to who we'd want—so we figured there's no point in paying for a will."

"Well," I replied, "if you want to be a pain in the a** from the grave, that's a great plan." I went on to explain that just because things *might* end up where you want eventually doesn't mean it'll be simple or smooth. Without a will, your loved ones could face a drawn-out legal process, unnecessary costs, and uncertainty during an already heartbreaking time. A will doesn't just decide where things go—it gives your family clear direction and one less thing to worry about when everything else feels upside down.

What Is a Will?

A will is a legal document that outlines who will inherit your assets after you pass away—these individuals are your beneficiaries. While your will is the "who gets your stuff when you die" document most people think of, it is also the document you will use to appoint:

- An executor to carry out the instructions in your will.
- Guardians for your children or pets, if applicable.
- Instructions for handling your remains after your passing.

Do I Need a Will?

If you're alive and don't have a will yet, the answer is yes. The value of a will isn't just about the document itself—it's about the important conversations you'll have, the decisions you'll make, and the **additional documents** you'll create during the estate planning process.

Estate planning is the process of thinking through your wishes and putting things in order for what happens after you pass away. A basic estate plan includes a few key documents, each with a distinct purpose. Here are some of the most common ones:

Power of Attorney (POA)

- A **financial power of attorney** allows someone you trust to manage your money and property if you're alive but unable to do so yourself. This authority ends when you pass away.

- A **medical power of attorney** authorizes someone you trust to make healthcare decisions on your behalf if you're unable to do so, such as choosing treatments or communicating with doctors.

Medical Directive

Also known as a **living will** or **advance directive**, this document outlines your medical wishes, such as:

- The interventions or treatments you want (or don't want).

- Whether you want to be an organ donor.

- Who you'd like to be allowed to visit you.

- Whether you'd like a member of your faith community to visit.

A medical directive provides clarity, sparing your loved ones from guessing what you would want during a stressful and emotional time. Allow me to share a real-life story to illustrate the importance of having a medical POA and a medical directive, even if you're young and healthy.

Terri's Story

At just 26, Terri Schiavo collapsed from cardiac arrest and suffered severe brain damage due to lack of oxygen. She never regained consciousness. Her husband believed she wouldn't have wanted to be kept alive in that condition and asked to have her feeding tube removed. Her parents disagreed and fought to keep her on life support. What followed was a painful 15-year legal battle that made national headlines.

The heartbreaking part? It all could have been avoided— if Terri had documented her medical wishes and chosen a medical power of attorney, her family would have had clear guidance and been spared years of emotional and legal turmoil.

How Do You Start?

Best: Work with an Attorney

Working with an attorney is the most reliable way to create a comprehensive estate plan. Attorneys can guide you through each step, answer your questions, and ensure that your documents comply with the estate laws in your state. They can also coordinate the presence of witnesses or a notary for the signing process.

Hiring an attorney becomes more important as you have more wealth, children, or complex family dynamics. Pricing varies based on your unique situation, the number of documents you need, and the attorney's qualifications. This approach provides peace of mind that everything should be handled correctly. I'll share some advice on hiring an attorney in the following chapter on building your "Dream Team".

Good: Online Will Program

Online programs such as Trust & Will or LegalZoom are affordable, accessible options that don't require scheduling with an attorney during business hours. These programs typically provide educational content to teach you about estate planning, but it's your responsibility to determine how that information applies to your unique situation.

At this price point, you probably won't be working directly with an attorney—more likely you'll be filling out templated forms. You'll need to arrange your own witnesses or notary when you sign. Keep in mind that estate law can change frequently, so choose a program that stays up to date.

Better than Nothing: Doing It Yourself

A mentor of mine used to joke that writing your wishes on the back of a napkin was better than nothing. While this won't be legally enforceable, the process of putting your thoughts in writing, even on a napkin, allows you to think through your wishes so your family has an idea of what they are. Just know this "back of the napkin" method is only a temporary stopgap. This might help your family guess your wishes in a pinch—but it's not legally enforceable. Don't stop here.

Worst: Leave It for Your Loved Ones

Doing nothing puts all the burden of making decisions and jumping through legal hoops onto your loved ones during an already difficult time. I understand that it's hard to think about death, and you're right— it's unlikely that you'll die anytime soon. But you just don't know.

Just like no one wakes up expecting to get in a car accident but still gets auto insurance, we don't expect to die but must still make it a priority to get our affairs in order.

Probate

Probate is the legal procedure that your estate goes through after you pass away. During probate, a court oversees the distribution of your estate to the proper heirs. Having a will simplifies and speeds up this process by providing clear instructions on how your assets should be handled.

As part of probate, the court authorizes your executor to:

- Pay all outstanding debts and taxes.

- Distribute the remaining property according to your will.

Once these tasks are completed, your estate is considered settled and the probate process is closed.

Avoiding Probate for Certain Assets

Some assets can skip the probate process altogether–saving time, money, and stress for your loved ones–by naming beneficiaries directly on the account.

- Retirement accounts like 401(k)s and IRAs, along with life insurance policies, usually require you to **name a beneficiary**. These assets are passed directly to that person and do not go through probate.

- You can also add a **Transfer on Death** (TOD) designation to nonretirement investments or bank accounts. This lets the funds go straight to your chosen beneficiary, giving them quicker access to cash—often helpful for covering immediate expenses.

- Another option is setting up a **trust**. Assets titled in the name of a trust bypass probate altogether and can be distributed according to your instructions, providing more privacy and control than beneficiary designations alone.

PRO TIP

The beneficiary listed on your account *overrides* anything written in your will. Make sure you keep both updated anytime your circumstances change.

What Is the Difference Between a Trust and a Will?

Wills and trusts are similar in that they both say who gets your assets, but they differ in how and when they take effect. A **will** only goes into effect after you pass away. It's generally a simpler document that allows you to:

- Name guardians for kids and pets.
- Designate where your assets go.
- Specify your final arrangements.

A **trust**, on the other hand, is effective immediately upon creation. Trusts are more complex but offer several additional benefits:

- They provide more control over when and how your assets are distributed.
- They help avoid probate, which can save time and money.

- They keep your estate matters private, as trusts do not become public records like wills.

Some people use both: a will to name guardians and a trust to manage assets and avoid probate. To fund a trust, you must **name the trust as the beneficiary** on your accounts and **transfer ownership of assets into the trust.** Without this step, the trust won't serve its purpose.

Mom and Dad

If you're unsure where your parents' documents are—or if they have any—now might be the time to ask. If the topic hasn't come up yet, going through the estate planning process for yourself may prepare you to have that conversation with them. You could say something like:

"Hey, Mom and Dad, I just finished making a will and medical directive, and it got me thinking—I'm not sure what your wishes are. Have you ever documented them? Where would I find those documents if I needed to?"

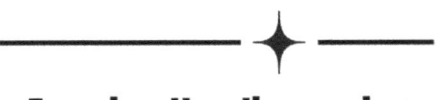

Framing the discussion around honoring their wishes can make the conversation easier for everyone involved.

Estate planning can be a sensitive subject. If you choose to bring up the conversation, make it clear that you're wanting to make sure your parents' wishes are honored, not digging for clues as to what you might inherit. Framing the discussion around honoring their wishes can make the conversation easier for everyone involved.

CHAPTER WRAP-UP

Key Takeaways

- If you're alive, you need a basic estate plan—including a will.

- Dying without a will or medical directive forces your loved ones to make tough decisions without guidance and requires them to jump through unnecessary hoops.

- The beneficiary you name on your account overrides any named beneficiaries in your will.

- Starting your own estate plan can be a powerful way to spark conversation with your parents or other loved ones.

Key Actions

- Get a will done.

- Complete a medical directive.

- Choose your executor and powers of attorney (POAs).

- Ensure your executor and POAs know where to find your documents.

- Review and update the beneficiaries on all of your accounts.

Journal Prompts

- What values or messages do you want to pass on through your estate planning?

- How do you feel about discussing your estate plans with your loved ones?

- What legacy do you hope to leave—financially, relationally, or spiritually?

"Alone, we can do so little; together, we can do so much."

—Helen Keller

Chapter 12

DREAM TEAM

Building Your Dream Team

The goal of this book is to help you create a financial foundation that you can build on. Throughout these chapters, we've only scratched the surface of each topic. To truly level up, you'll need to dive deeper–ideally with the support of your own dream team.

Your dream team is the collection of people who will help you on your financial journey. They provide education and insight, as well as support and encouragement.

In this chapter we'll identify key roles your team should include and help you figure out who is best suited to fill them.

Friends

While you'll need professionals on your dream team, the place to start is the people who you spend the most time with—your friends. Perhaps you've heard the *saying, "Show me your friends and I'll show you your future,"* or *"You become the average of the five people you spend the most time with."* In other words, your friends significantly influence your mindset and habits.

Do your friends encourage you to live intentionally, celebrate your successes, and help you work towards your goals? Friends like these will help you grow and move forward with your life.

Alternatively, if your friends allow you to play the victim and focus on what's beyond your control or encourage habits that conflict with your goals— like overspending—they may hold you back.

It's going to be really difficult to change your financial patterns while surrounded by friends who don't want you to change. You don't necessarily need to end the friendships, but you'll want to be really intentional about who is in your innermost circle, and who you spend the most time with.

Therapist

A therapist can help you navigate the thoughts, beliefs, and emotions that surface as you work through financial material. You may now be aware of money triggers you hadn't noticed before, and a therapist can help you create proactive strategies to respond to them.

If you want to do some deep work around your money baggage, you may consider finding a financial therapist. Financial therapy provides a safe space to explore your money stories and behaviors, empowering you to work through and move past them.

DREAM TEAM

Financial Advisor

A financial advisor can play a key role on your dream team, helping you with one of the most intimate and vulnerable parts of your life—your money. Because money is personal, you'll want to find someone you trust and feel comfortable with.

What Kind of Financial Advisors Are There?

The title "Financial Advisor" is used to describe a range of financial professionals. The following are specific types of financial advisors:

Investment Manager: Helps you grow your money by selecting and managing investments based on your financial goals and risk tolerance. Their focus is on long-term growth.

Financial Planner: Offers holistic financial guidance, from retirement planning to saving for goals like homeownership and paying off debt. Financial planners can also help you determine how much insurance you need.

Insurance Broker: We'll cover insurance agents later in this chapter, but I want to address the fact that there are insurance brokers who present themselves as financial advisors, but they may not be licensed to sell investments or manage portfolios. They often rely solely on insurance products, like annuities or whole life policies, to help you reach your investment goals. These tools can be useful in certain situations, but they might not be the best fit for your needs. I'll share some helpful questions you can ask in the Insurance Agent section of the chapter.

How Do Financial Advisors Get Paid?

Understanding how your advisor gets paid helps ensure their recommendations align with your best interests. Common payment structures include:

- **Asset Management Fee:** An annual fee for managing your investments, usually charged as a percentage of your account balance. For example, a 1% fee on a $10,000 account would cost $100 per year, typically deducted monthly or quarterly.

- **Commission:** A sales charge for investments or insurance products. For instance, if you invest $10,000 with a 5% commission, $9,500 is invested while $500 covers the sales fee. Commissions aren't inherently bad, but it's important to ensure the advisor is recommending products because they're a good fit for you, not just to earn an upfront commission or because these are the only products they are able to sell.

- **Financial Planning Fee:** A flat fee charged for creating a financial plan, either as a package or hourly rate. This fee is paid upfront or over time and is not necessarily tied to the value of your assets (though your net worth may be a factor in how much you pay). If an advisor is offering you free financial planning, just know that they likely intend to make their money by selling their investment or insurance services.

Questions to Ask

When choosing a financial advisor, asking the right questions can help ensure they are the best fit for your needs. Here are key topics to cover:

1. **Do you have an investment minimum or minimum planning fee?**

   Some advisors require clients to have a certain amount of assets to invest or charge a minimum fee for their services. Make sure their requirements align with your financial situation.

2. **What licenses do you hold?**

   Understanding an advisor's qualifications is essential to know what services they can provide. Common licenses include:

   - **Series 7:** Allows the advisor to buy and sell a wide range of investment products, such as stocks and bonds. It also demonstrates knowledge of industry regulations.

   - **Series 66:** Builds on the Series 7 by adding state law knowledge and the ability to act as both a securities agent and an investment advisor. This combination offers broader qualifications.

   - **Series 6:** Authorizes the advisor to sell specific products like mutual funds and variable annuities. It is less comprehensive than the Series 7 but still demonstrates expertise in these areas.

   - **Insurance Licenses**: Advisors may hold licenses to sell life, health, disability, home, or auto insurance. Since the tools they offer can vary, it's important to ask about the types of insurance products they can provide.

3. How will we communicate?

Communication is a common pain point in client-advisor relationships. Ask about:

- **Response times:** How quickly can you expect a reply to emails or phone calls?

- **Accessibility:** Can you schedule a call for urgent questions?

- **Direct contact:** Will you work directly with the advisor you meet, or will your relationship transition to a team member?

- **Meeting preferences:** Does the advisor offer both virtual meetings and in-person meetings? Are you limited to a certain number of meetings per year?

4. Can you share how you've helped clients similar to me?

This question gives you insight into the advisor's experience and whether they've worked with clients who share your goals or challenges. It's an opportunity to gauge how their expertise aligns with your specific needs.

Money/Budget Coach

A money coach helps you improve your financial habits by setting goals, creating budgets, and making smarter decisions about spending and saving. Unlike a financial advisor, who focuses on investments, a money coach specializes in everyday money management and behavioral change.

They cannot make investment recommendations or manage investments for you.

Questions to Ask

- What philosophies do you apply to your coaching?

- How do you charge for your services?

- Can you share examples of how you've helped other clients like me?

- How often will we meet?

- What happens if I have questions between our meetings?

Accountant

Accountants provide tax advice and assist with filing tax returns. They ensure you're withholding the right amount of taxes from your paycheck and help plan for any amounts owed. If you have self-employment income or own a business, an accountant can be a trusted partner in keeping your records accurate, staying on top of regulations, and finding opportunities to save money at tax time.

Questions to Ask

- What types of clients do you typically work with?

- How do you charge for your services, and what's included in your fee structure?

- How do you stay updated on tax laws and regulations that might impact me?

- Can you help me make the most of tax deductions and credits specific to my situation?

Insurance Agent

Insurance agents help you choose the right insurance policies and coverage levels for your needs. They explain what each policy covers, its cost, and why you might need it. Some agents are captive, which means they work for a single insurance company and can only offer that company's products.Brokers, on the other hand, can work with multiple companies to find you the best options.

Questions to Ask

- What types of insurance policies do you specialize in?

- Do you work independently with multiple companies, or are you tied to one insurer? How does that affect the choices available to me?

- How do you ensure your recommendations align with my financial goals and budget?

- What is your process for reviewing and updating my policies as my needs change?

Mortgage Lender

Mortgage lenders help you apply for a home loan or access your home equity. They assess your credit score, income, and debts to determine your loan eligibility, interest rates, and repayment terms. Their role is to guide you through the process and help you secure a mortgage that fits your budget and needs.

You may consider meeting with a lender in advance to give yourself time to boost your credit and create a smoother path to homeownership.

Questions to Ask

- What types of loans do you specialize in?

- What are the current interest rates, and how do you determine the best rate I qualify for?

- What fees are involved in the loan process, and can you provide a detailed breakdown?

- Do you offer preapproval, and how long does it typically take?

- How will you communicate throughout the loan process, and what can I expect in terms of timelines?

Real Estate Agent

Real estate agents assist with buying, selling, or renting properties. They have deep knowledge of local markets, property values, and legal requirements, guiding you from the initial search to closing the deal. They also negotiate on your behalf to get the best possible terms.

Questions to Ask

- Can you share an example of how you helped a buyer (or seller) like me navigate a difficult transaction?

- What services do you offer beyond buying and selling?

- Do you work on your own or as part of a team?

- What is your process for helping clients find the best property within their budget?

- What is your availability, and how do you communicate with clients during the buying or selling process?

Estate Planning Attorney

An estate planning attorney specializes in helping you create legal documents like wills, trusts, powers of attorney, and advance healthcare directives. Their role is to make sure your wishes are clearly documented, your assets are transferred according to your plan, and your loved ones are protected from unnecessary legal headaches, taxes, or disputes. A good estate planning attorney not only drafts the documents but also explains your options in plain language and helps you think through decisions you may not have considered, such as guardianship for children or long-term care planning.

Questions to Ask

- What is your experience with estate planning, and do you regularly handle cases like mine?

- Do you recommend a will, a trust, or both for my situation, and why?

- How do you charge flat fee or hourly for your services, and what's included in that cost?

- How often should I update my estate plan, and do you offer ongoing services to help with that?

Asking for Referrals

If you don't already know professionals to consider, asking friends or family for recommendations can be a great starting point. Use these questions to evaluate whether their recommended professional is a good fit for your needs:

How do you know this person, and have you worked with them personally? If so, for how long?

You want to make sure that your friend is referring to this professional to you because they're good at what they do, not just because they're personal friends or in a referral group together. And if they do work with this professional personally, you want to make sure they've had enough experience to vet the person.

What products or services do they provide?

Even if someone is good at what they do, if what they do isn't what you need, their expertise won't be very helpful. For example, a financial advisor specializing in tax efficiencies for high-net-worth clients might not be a fit if you're mostly looking for help with paying down debt and changing your spending patterns.

How do they communicate with you, and how accessible are they?

Does this person proactively communicate with their clients, sharing important updates and helping them take advantage of new opportunities? Do they check in regularly to make sure that what's been set up is still a good fit? How quickly can you reach them if you have an important question? When you do reach them, do they communicate in a way that's easily understood? Some professionals, while brilliant, may lack emotional intelligence or have poor communication habits like using overly technical language.

How much does it cost to work with them?

You have to be careful here, as fees are subject to change over time, and your friend's situation may be met with a different price point than yours. Still, getting an idea of how much it *might* cost to work with them can help you feel more comfortable reaching out to them.

Do they make space for emotions?

Money is often an emotional topic. Finding a professional who can engage with or hold space for those feelings can be important, especially if you anticipate needing support during challenging moments.

Why Ask These Questions?

These questions can give you valuable insights into whether the professional might provide you with the same positive experience your friend has had. They'll also help you identify red flags or mismatched expectations before committing to a working relationship.

CHAPTER WRAP-UP

Key Takeaways

- You need a supportive team to help you continue learning and growing.
- Ask strategic questions to make sure you find someone who is a good fit for you and your situation.
- If you get a referral from a friend or family member, ask a few questions to confirm that the professional is also likely to be a good fit for you.

Key Actions

- Start building your "dream team" by reaching out to professionals for interviews.

Journal Prompts

Who do you already have in your life who could be a positive member of your "dream team"?

How have the people in your life already been acting as members of your "dream team"?

REFERENCES

Stanny, B. (2002). *Secrets of Six-Figure Women: Surprising strategies to up your earnings and change your life*. HarperBusiness.

Experian 2022

Gender Pay Gap: https://www.pewresearch.org/short-reads/2023/03/01/gender-pay-gap-facts/

Financial Abuse: https://money.usnews.com/credit-cards/articles/survey-nearly-22-experienced-financial-abuse-in-a-past-relationship#:~:text=Survey%20Highlights,re%20unsure%20if%20they%20are

Renters Insurance: https://www.safehome.org/home-insurance/renters-insurance-market-report/

ABOUT THE AUTHOR

Nicole Burdick, known as *The Money Maven*, is a financial advisor, author, and speaker with more than a decade of experience helping women make smart, values-driven financial decisions. She is the founder of Money Maven Financial, a female-centered financial planning and investment management firm dedicated to empowering women—and the men who support them—through education, clarity, and confidence.

Nicole is currently pursuing her master's degree in Financial Planning at Kansas State University, expanding her expertise in behavioral finance and financial therapy to better serve her clients. Her professional journey has grown into a deeply impactful career focused on guiding women to align their financial choices with their values and long-term goals.

Her insights have been featured in both local and national publications, and she is a sought-after speaker for both business organizations and community groups. A committed community leader, Nicole has served on the board of Whatcom Women in Business, where she has played an active role in supporting local nonprofits and raising scholarship funds for women pursuing higher education.

When she isn't working, Nicole enjoys spending time with her husband and their two children riding bikes and exploring parks in their hometown of Bellingham, Washington. She also enjoys writing music and performing at open mics locally.

The Money Maven Manual is Nicole's debut book, combining practical financial strategies with personal storytelling and guided reflection. Written in a voice that is both professional and approachable, it equips readers to rewrite their money stories, clarify their values, and design financial lives they genuinely love.